How to eat a
FAILURE
SANDWICH

An Entrepreneur's Guide to Failure – A Memoir

PHIL BURKS

FLUENCY
TELLING STORIES THAT MATTER

Produced with the assistance of Fluency Organization, Inc.

Interior by Inkwell Creative

Genesis PULSE® is a registered trademark of GenCore Candeo, Ltd and Phil
Burks, Tyler, Texas.

FIRST iZ® is a registered trademark of GenCore Candeo, Ltd and Burks
GenCore, Inc., Tyler, Texas, and is licensed to Phirst Technologies, LLC.

WAZE® is a registered trademark of Waze Mobile Ltd, Israel and Google, LLC,
Mountain View, California.

Motorola and Motorola Solutions® are trademarks of Motorola Trademark
Holdings, LLC, Chicago, Illinois.

How to Eat a Failure Sandwich is the Swiss Army knife of books. I found it to be packed full of humor, life lessons, historic reminders, a primer on the evolution of technology, inspiration, business acumen, and leadership insights. Burks has filled these pages with wisdom, and you're sure to benefit significantly from reading and reflecting on his words.

Brian Brandt
CEO, Core Insights

I will never look at another sandwich the same after reading Phil's book. I met Phil because of our common love for a particular motorcycle called the Can Am Spyder. I could see a curiosity and drive as he would show mods (modifications) he was doing to Darth (his Spyder). Here, he tells some of the stories that go behind that curiosity and how failure drove him forward. As a fellow entrepreneur and friend, I've learned why Phil and I get along and have a mutual care and respect for each other. I've been self-employed since 1986 and have had my share of failures in life and business. I've also done many things that were said can't be done. Phil shares the passion for filling voids we all didn't know we had.

I'm sure many who read this book will be inspired to keep pushing forward when things are not looking promising. Phil and I have shared many of these sandwiches throughout our lives! His love of technology and doing things right has been a motivator for me, including his generosity. If you know Phil, you can say, "I know a good man." Looking forward to sharing this meal of life with others.

Lamont Bryden
Founder, Lamonster Garage

I've known Phil Burks as a friend, a brother in Christ, and a fellow servant of the Lord for over three decades. We have literally traveled around the world sharing the good news of Jesus. I can recall the days when Genesis was a struggling company— beset with failures. But I always knew that because of Phil's grit, determination, and faith, he would lead the company from the flat line of failure into the stratosphere of success.

For anyone who aspires to excellent leadership skills, *How to Eat a Failure Sandwich* is a must read. Phil employs humor and utilizes delightful gastronomical metaphors to emphasize that there's only one way to eat a Failure Sandwich: one bite at a time. You'll laugh while you learn about the value of mistakes. Phil's key thought is that failure is never fatal, nor final. As long as a person keeps dreaming and refuses to give up, even the sky isn't the limit. God specializes in turning setbacks into comebacks, and God is using Phil Burks to spread this message. I highly encourage you to read this book and give a copy to everyone in your organization.

Pastor David O. Dykes
Green Acres Baptist Church
Tyler, Texas

I turned my back on God long before I met Phil Burks. Mine was not the case of an irreconcilable suffering. Rather, mine was rooted in the original sin itself. I craved to be my own god. I craved control. I was engrossed with my own intellect. Defending my atheistic beliefs and lifestyle was easy, given man's ignorance of God's mystery. Like Robert Robinson, composer of the cherished hymn, "Come, Though Fount of Every Blessing," I once relished opportunities to heckle Christians. Their hypocrisy was low-hanging fruit, and their inability to defend a blind faith was an enjoyable debate. But also like Robinson, "Jesus sought me when a stranger." Phil crossed my path in 2004, and we became fast friends on the common ground of technology and business. The two most irritating things about him were that he actually lived out what he believed, and that he wasn't afraid to say, "I don't know the answer to that, but I know God." Over time, Phil's unwavering faith and his intimate relationship with Christ left its mark on me. Secretly, I was weary from years of self-inflicted pain. At first, I questioned. Then, I listened. And finally, I heard. What my soul truly craved was "streams of mercy, never ceasing." Because of Phil Burks, I knew where that stream flowed from.

Micheal Lavender

Friend, "numbers-whisperer," former atheist, and a "prone to wander" child of God

I met Phil Burks at a Can Am Spyder rally in Springfield, Missouri, in 2013. He is a brother in Christ and a fellow electrical nerd. He is an entrepreneur—I'm a pastor. Oh, how I have loved reading his book. It is him! Although it is hard to imagine most of his hardships, knowing the guy he is now, he told me the story of his opportunity in Nashville while we were looking at the "Batman" building in Nashville together! This book should encourage all who read it to persevere, to push forward through failure, and to succeed when the odds are against you. Life is hard, at best.

Phil also introduced me to Bernie, what a precious man of God. Phil and Bobbie have hosted my wife and me in their home, and they have been in our home! What a great friend, encourager, and witness for our Lord Jesus. I'm proud to call him my friend. Although I don't think we can say we're finished until we've heard the words, "Well done, my good and faithful servant" from our Lord, Phil is a winner and a true friend, and I hope I get to stand with Phil and hear those words together!

Pastor Dale Lawing

Kings Mountain, North Carolina

Former Duke Energy Project Manager

Loved the book! Very entertaining. As a fellow entrepreneur, I totally related to the stories and loved the analogies that Phil used in the book. I wish my husband and I would have had this book to read when we were going through our own Colossal and Seven-Year Ick. This book is a great investment for any aspiring entrepreneur or someone in the middle of the journey. Being in business for yourself is like an emotional rollercoaster ride, and having a healthy perspective and tolerance for the ride is crucial. This book provides the reader with an overview of the life of a business and how the tough times must be viewed as "learning opportunities." Everything happens for a reason, whether positive or negative. An important part of the journey is when you take time to step back and reflect on the purpose behind those difficult times. Phil wrote the book in an easy-to-read style, which made it fun and interesting. It didn't read like a "business book" but simply a powerful story that anyone would enjoy.

Lisa M. Lujan
Co-Founder, Mentoring Minds, LLC

Like R.G. LeTourneau, the founder of LeTourneau University, Phil didn't quit in the face of adversity. Mr. LeTourneau is known for his hundreds of patents and the creation of the world's giant machines, but the general public never witnessed the thousands of hours and the failures along the way that led to his success. As a student at LeTourneau University, Phil saw Mr. LeTourneau's entrepreneurial spirit and heart for sharing the Good News of Jesus to the world. It is that spirit that he captures in *How to Eat a Failure Sandwich*!

Steven D. Mason, Ph.D.
President, LeTourneau University
Longview, Texas

I first met Phil when he was a young boy. I am the guy who gave him his first ride in an airplane (and the rest is history, so to speak!). I knew his parents before Phil existed and even before they knew each other. I see much of them reflected in these pages. Reconnecting with Phil after 55 years is one of the highlights of my 88+ years. It was a joy to fill in the gaps of how God worked in their lives and to see His grace working from one generation to another. Yes, life is often "messy," but Phil shows that with prayer, perseverance, and the power of God, all things are possible.

Bernie May, Sr.
Founder, Seed Company
Former President, Wycliffe Bible Translators
Former President, JAARS

People who make their living with the pen tend to be guarded and rethink their words. Those who aren't writers don't know how to write any other way than to lay out the unguarded truth. So goes, *How to Eat a Failure Sandwich*. The irony of this honest-to-the-bone autobiography is that Burks is completely open about how cautious and guarded he's been during his life. And how you can learn from his experiences. Early in his story, he talks of taking radios apart to see how they allow communication. In this book, he takes the different chapters of his life apart to reveal his communication with God and the periods of deafening silence. This book is a must-read for any young person with ambition. Combine ambition with Burks' life lessons and you'll have the ingredients to make your sandwich a tasty one.

John Moore
Author

In this well-crafted tale—told, no doubt, with the story-telling skills the author hammered out on the anvil of his hilarious mishaps as a young radio DJ and TV broadcaster—Phil Burks gives us an authentic and entertaining portrait of how to roll with the punches, how to accept, examine, and learn from failure, and how to eventually win at this thing we call life. And importantly, the reader is reminded that winning is rightfully defined as leading a life focused on pursuing your God-given purpose. *How to Eat a Failure Sandwich* is a quick, yet meaty, gem!

    Wade Myers

    Investor and Entrepreneur

There is a whole category of resources today portraying God as a snowplow removing all the obstacles and impediments in our lives. This is not one of those books. This is the story of a man (and a friend) who has persevered through the setbacks, failures, and mistakes of a real life. Albert Einstein said it best: "Adversity introduces a man to himself." Phil takes us with him from his early years of a charmed life to times of disappointment, being stuck, tempted to give up and along the way discovering one of the great lessons of life: God is preparing us in each experience for faithfulness through every trial, as well as each success. There are circumstances and changes we don't choose, but we face them and that is the beginning of giving up charm for true courage. This is a very personal story of what it means to grow in Christ. It is a privilege to journey with him.

    Fred Smith

    Founder, The Gathering

I found *How to Eat a Failure Sandwich* was, in a number of cases, similar to my own personal experiences and evoked like emotions. While not easy at the time, it is easy to look back and appreciate the hardships, along with the eventual successes. Phil's openness made this a compelling read, and I found myself flashing back and forth from Phil's life story to my own. Once I started reading, I was immersed in Phil's heartbreaking stories, only to be rallied back by faith and ultimate success. Comparatively, I became more appreciative of my own struggles and how they shaped my life. I appreciate learning more about my friend Phil Burks and his testimony of faith. More importantly, I believe this is a great read for younger people to help them understand the full breadth of life and to reinforce the fact that one must never give up and instead look at failure as an opportunity to learn and let God direct their lives. I have always believed that there is a purpose for our lives, but we must be willing to be open to the opportunities. The book is interesting, engaging, heartbreaking, and heartwarming, and everyone will benefit from Phil's life story. I still want to know who of the "two" was kicked out of school. I now appreciate Phil even more as a friend, visionary, and man of faith!

    Charles Werner
    Fire Chief Emeritus (Ret)
    Charlottesville, Virginia
    Founder, DroneResponders.org

The American Dream often includes some nightmares along the way. If you can stay the course, you learn to cherish the latter in pursuit of the former. Phil Burks has done that very thing. Phil not only documents in *How to Eat a Failure Sandwich* what it means to be a successful entrepreneur, but also what it means to be a successful human being.

    Jason Wright
    Founder, Texas Titan Media

To the young business dreamers.
Phail phuriously, but never ever quit.

Acknowledgements

This is dangerous territory. I know I'm going to forget or not mention someone, due to space and having to draw a line somewhere, and thus raise a question. As this is my first book, my list is very, very long. Many names are mentioned throughout the book. These are people who have had a profound influence and meant so much in my life to this point, including my "Best Friend" (you'll find him as you read).

But here I go...

Dr. Bobbie Burks, my bride. You have dogged determination—working over six years to get your Ph.D., just because you wanted to keep your brain active. You are an amazing person, and I admire you on so many levels. Thank you for your constant encouragement, for believing in me, and for not quitting on me, even when I am such a sloppy sandwich. You've traveled the world with me, and now we ryde the nation together on our Spyders. I love you. Ecclesiastes 4:9-12

My kids: Jenny, Mandy, Ally, Josh. Each of you has made me a better person. As I wrote this book, I saw in my life a lot of the intensity and anger Dad had in his early life. I know I've apologized over the years for how I've been too harsh at times as your dad. I truly am sorry for those times. But in spite of those dark times, ALL of you have turned out to be more amazing and better than I ever was or will be. Psalm 127:3-5

Joyce and Shirley, my sisters. Readers will discover some of their story in this book about how for 30 of my years I really didn't understand who they were! But I can say that for the last 38 years, they truly ARE my sisters. They helped fill in so much history and get it right.

Mike Parks, my friend. Mike only gets one mention in the book, but he has encouraged, listened, advised, and pushed me for as long as we have known each other. We have laughed until we couldn't breathe and cried until there were no more tears. We've collaborated and created spectacular things to help tell the Good News. He even once loaned me $350 to fly to see Motorola once when I had no money to go! Proverbs 17:17

Neil Fichthorn, mentor. Neil gets a few mentions, but the story where he made such an impact happened when I was a high school kid. He called me to the front of a Sunday school class to do a little acting, speaking one of the soliloquies in *King Arthur*. That single act of admiration lit a fire in me.

Jim Nipp, Genesis President. You have taken our

company to heights that I never dreamed possible. You have assembled and pastored a team of over-achievers who create software solutions to help our first responders be heroes. I can sleep at night, full well knowing it is in your hands. Thank you.

Bernie May, Founder of Seed Company. You're never too old to find a mentor. On December 2, 2016, we reconnected. I was 64 and he was 84. In four short years you elevated my spiritual and business life to new heights. I thank God for you constantly because without you and your parents, I would not be here.

I KNOW I am missing dear friends who have had great influence on my life. Do know that when I get to heaven, my mind will be clear and I'll thank you then!

I do want to thank the six or so crowdsourced proofreaders who read the manuscript in breakneck time to look for anything glaring. This is a relatively new concept in publishing, and since I rarely do anything "normal," I liked the idea! You have saved yet another failure I might have needed to write about!

And I need to acknowledge Mary Ann Lackland, the CEO of Fluency. She set the pace, asked the hard questions, brought out memories, and wove random stories into valuable lessons. She has been an encourager when I was hurting from writing the difficult stories captured here, reminding me that you would someday be reading these stories at just the right time in your life.

Table of Contents

Preface   19

ONE   The Sloppy Joe   25

TWO   The B-L-T   49

THREE   The East Texas Grinder   69

FOUR   The Patty Melt   93

FIVE   The Colossal   121

SIX   The Seven-Year Ick   135

SEVEN   The Looky Loo   161

EIGHT   The Regret on Rye   183

NINE   The Double Decker Doozy   213

TEN   When Failure Tastes Good   231

Story Index   257

About the Author   261

Additional Resources   263

Preface

I flunked typing in high school.

Even when I took it again in summer school, I snuck by with a "mercy" D from my teacher, which contributed to my overall 2.8 GPA. I am still a horrible typist. I use three fingers on my left hand and two on my right. Somehow I have written hundreds of thousands of emails and even authored a few detailed software manuals. Never in a million years did I dream I would write a book. As you will learn, I don't think I'm that interesting. I don't have a profit motive to write a book, and I certainly didn't have the time to do all of the work.

But three things hit home through this process. First, Fluency Organization, Inc. has hit on a formula for making a book like this come to life. The CEO and I talked for about an hour, once per week, for almost a year. Mary Ann prompted me to tell stories, asked the hard questions, and guided the content kind of like a sculptor who cuts away all the unnecessary stuff in the block of marble to reveal the resultant work of art. We really weren't sure at first what the result would be, or the title for that matter, until we were over 50% complete. Mary Ann organized my thoughts and stories, typed them up (yippee!), I edited and helped fill in blanks, and the result is what you are holding. Sixty-eight years of learning lessons and one year distilling them.

The second element I learned was that the process caused me to dig out memories that I had forgotten. Some were stashed away in my mind because they are so painful. Others were captured on dozens of letters my dad wrote over the years. In fact, some of the stories that I THOUGHT I knew, were not confirmed until I went back to newspaper archives to get the truth. There has always been a piece of me that was afraid I would forget important things. I wanted to write a book to capture the stories and memories in print before they leaked from my brain. I've been reminded by others throughout this process that I am a lot like my dad, since they got to know him through my eyes reading these pages. They're right. Dad captured much of his life banging out letters on manual typewriters throughout the last 30 years he was alive. Maybe he too feared he would forget. He lived to the age of 92, and his mind remained sharp. I'm not taking that chance!

The third big takeaway is how much I have learned through many failures. I realized that I have stories to tell that someone else can read and relate to. And I've learned far more from my wrong turns than my glowing successes. Who knows? Maybe someone will keep pushing through a difficult time because they see that I've been there, too, and I came out on the other side of it. As one of my mentors once told me, failure is not part of your identity. It is part of your *journey*. It's just ONE chapter in your greater story.

We have crafted my failure stories into business lessons for the budding entrepreneur, as well as life lessons for the average person. I suppose I never thought of using my failures to help others. But in the past seven years, I have found myself mentoring business-minded people, both young and old. Some, actually many, are seeking career changes. Others are trying to understand how to be successful. These meetings helped me learn that I had something in my history that might have value to someone else. My passion for taking apart radios as a child turned out to be a transferable skill that parlayed not only into a career but also helped me in my role as a mentor. When people come to me for advice, I approach their concerns the same way I approached old radios. I can take apart and analyze business ideas and positions for entrepreneurs and business owners and then help them put it all back together again in a way that makes sense.

While some of the events in this book are worthy of being a made-for-TV movie, if I do say so myself, we had to avoid details due to non-disclosure agreements and/or to protect business interests. You may find your story in here and say that it's not how you remember the events! Just know that I've tried to do my best to capture everything as accurately as possible and from my point of view. That's my loving way of saying, "Hey—feel free to write a book and tell your side!"

And one final thing.

I also learned how much my faith and belief system has guided and helped me and is now helping others. I realize that some readers will share my belief in God and his son Jesus. I also fully understand that many of you will be quite the opposite. I know a dear friend will read this book, and he was an agnostic and borderline atheist for a large part of his life. When we would go to lunch every two or three weeks, I would ask if it was okay for me to ask a blessing on the food. We have a high respect for each other, despite our belief differences, and most times he gave a gesture saying, "Sure, go ahead." He would sit quietly while I asked God for a simple blessing (not pressuring him in any way or trying to save the world). But I would end the prayers with, "...in Jesus' name I pray, amen. Just in case I'm right!"

That's kind of how this book is. I am only telling my stories and my journey. There will be no pressure to believe like I do or to convert to some religion. By the way, I despise religion. As I hope you'll come to understand, what I have discovered in my faith is way different than religion. My faith is not a set of rules that, when broken, leads to punishment. That is why I call it a belief and a relationship, not religion.

If you've known me over the years, you might call me a rational, sane individual—and yet struggle with how I can really believe in a gracious God through all of this. That's the part I look forward to explaining most throughout this book. I don't shy away from the fact that my young life was changed when I asked Jesus to be my Best Friend. Nor do I sugarcoat the fact that the relationship I have with Jesus does not guarantee a happy, rosy life. But I do try to show how it all fits together.

Enjoy!
Phil

ONE

The Sloppy Joe

The first time my wife and I traveled to New York City, we did the regular tourist stuff. For tourists, New York is a place where sitting down to eat in a red vinyl booth of an iconic delicatessen like The Roxy is as much of a must-do as walking in Central Park. Eyeball any NYC deli menu, and you can't help but laugh at the creative and crazy names they give some of their signature creations. It's not just a hot pastrami—it's The Steaming Empire State Building. It's not a fish sandwich—it's The Carp-e Diem. (Get it?) It's not tidy cucumber sandwiches that New York is famous for. They're known for the wobbly tower of mustard-soaked lettuce, pickles, sauerkraut, egg, cheese, and slabs of meat between two bookends of bread holding a mess together. When I saw these monsters come out of the kitchen, they made the triple-decker Dagwood cartoon sandwich of my childhood seem boring. The server slaps this thing down in front of you, and you know you have a job to do for the next half-hour taking your time getting it down the hatch.

"How do you eat an elephant?" the old joke goes. Answer? "One bite at a time." How do you get through failure? It's hard, but I've learned that it's the same way you eat an elephant—or a New York deli sandwich. You get through failure and pain one bite, one day at a time.

I'm broadening the definition of "failure" for this book because "Failure Sandwiches" are served in a variety of ways in different phases of our lives. It can be an ongoing problem, a crisis, a disappointment, a mistake, or a painful season. What you DO after you fail is what matters most. You can't rush it any more than you can devour a NYC deli sandwich in the span of a 10-minute lunchbreak. You must take your time in life and learn all you can from the whole messy process.

So what is your strategy for getting through it when life serves you a Failure Sandwich? Do you push your chair away from the table and refuse to take a bite? Do you insist this is NOT what you ordered? Of course it's not what you wanted! But failure and disappointment happen to all of us, regardless of what we want. There's not much else to do but tuck your napkin under your chin, take a big bite, and start making your way through it to the end.

Whether you are just starting out, married or single, whether you are someone in transition between careers, or just someone struggling with a desire to do something new—but you're not sure what it is—I have the same message: Stay in the game. Take a sharp knife and a pocket dictionary and cut out the word "quit." You are not permitted to quit. You are not! You are, however, allowed to fail. Failure is fine. Changing directions is not defeat. Learning the hard way is not falling short, as long as you learn.

I have a rolling Word document with the illustrious file name, "Phil's Life Failures." I add to it every so often to keep it current. I've plowed through my share of Failure Sandwiches, and I'm not ashamed of failure. Okay, maybe a little bit. But one thing I hope my story makes clear is that mine has not been a road lined with unicorns and roses.

What I ended up doing with my life turned out to be much different than what I originally wanted to do. In almost 50 years of working in tech industries, I've made huge strides, and I've made ginormous mistakes. Lots of mistakes. I've gone full throttle, and there were weeks when I lost my mojo. I've failed in several business pursuits, and I've had many successes beyond my wildest dreams. My dad was a blue-collar factory worker who spent time in prison. My mom died of cancer. I was told

I was "stupid" as a child and that I would never amount to anything. I went through a divorce. I know the ins and outs of blended families. I've lost friends over my principles, had to make agonizing business decisions, and I know what it's like to run out of money before you run out of month. There was even a time when I lost my ability to dream because I was too busy just surviving day-to-day, worried sick that we weren't going to make it. When I decided to write this book, dozens of memories flooded my mind. In these pages, I've narrowed down my experiences to a few Failure Sandwiches I've somehow made my way through so far.

A FAMILY WITH HISTORY

When I was in college and dirt poor, my luxury on Wednesdays was a walk across the street to Bodacious BBQ for their Sloppy Joe special—three gooey ground meat and tomato sauce sandwiches for a dollar. I'd plop down my dollar and feel like a king. I loved them for several reasons, the least of which was licking my fingers to get the last morsel of goodness. But one of those reasons was that, even though they were a mess to eat, I felt very proud of myself after conquering three of those beasts.

I call this opening part of my life and my family's life The Sloppy Joe. Life is messy, if you haven't already figured that out. It's complicated and not easy to deal with—especially when it comes to families. Families are the quintessential Sloppy Joe, and my family history is sloppy by some measures.

Despite our protests, life serves up The Sloppy Joe—a sandwich that you eat slowly over time because it gets all over the place, no matter how hard you try. Just when you think you have a handle on it, chaos comes spilling out the sides and down your arm. In my case, whenever I'd ask Dad for details about portions of his past, he'd dismiss my curiosity or jokingly say he'd have to explain it when I was 18 or older. Only with every passing year, it became easier not to tell me (or just harder to tell me the truth). Life gets in the way sometimes of important things we know we ought to do or say, and we end up putting off priorities for a rainy day.

Maybe my parents never would have told me, I'm not sure. The only reason I discovered the real story of my family's past was because my life had started to mirror my father's in some eerie coincidences. Only I couldn't see the obvious because, unlike my other relatives who knew way more than I did, I didn't have the entire script of my dad's life before I came on the scene.

When I learned the truth about my father, I was a young man staring down the long, black barrel of a divorce—something I assumed would explode the vision my parents had of their reasonably perfect only son. The last thing on earth I wanted to do was to tell my parents that my first wife, Lee, and I were separated.

I was deeply ashamed, sitting alone and crying in my

living room night after night with the word "FAILURE" blazing in my mind. We had two beautiful daughters together, Jenny and Mandy—both under 10 years of age at that time. I felt irresponsible and berated myself. I simply could not believe I'd ended up as a young, single dad with a broken marriage so early in life.

When I finally got up the guts to stop by my parents' house one day to confess I was getting divorced, I felt sick inside. The words stuck in my throat as I informed them of the news. There was a long silence before my dad finally spoke up.

"Son, how much time do you have?" he asked me.

Confused, I told him I could spend all afternoon with them if need be.

"Good," he said. "Get comfortable. I have a story for you."

My father then began unraveling a tale so unbelievable that for the next two hours my eyebrows stayed arched and my eyes remained moist with tears.

LET'S PUT THIS IN CONTEXT

Some of what I'm telling here, I did not know until I was writing this book! My dad grew up near Lynchburg, Virginia, and my mother was from Chester, Pennsylvania, a suburb of Philadelphia. My dad was born Willie Baynard Burks in 1916. That's Willie, not William, although at some point he gave up the fight and just introduced himself as Bill. He went to work on the family farm early, starting in the family garden and advancing to harvesting corn and wheat. His 10 brothers and sisters worked together to put food on their large dinner table and also trade other crops with area farmers.

Along the way my dad learned to play the guitar, banjo, harmonica, and the 32-string Autoharp. Many evenings, much of the family would sing popular songs from the radio, crooning the tunes of The Carter Family or Jimmie Rodgers, the country music stars of the 1920s. He taught himself more and more songs and found that he had a knack for singing and performing.

Willie dreamed of something more for himself, something that would take him beyond the farming work that generations of Burks had spent their lifetimes doing. He worked various jobs until around 1939 when a relative told him of an opportunity with the rapidly growing steel industry in Pennsylvania. So my dad moved and learned the craft of the blast furnace, one of the most dangerous parts of a steel mill. He started as a repairman, learned most of the skilled labor jobs, and steadily rose into the supervision ranks. He recounted almost losing his life on several occasions.

In his spare time, he kept practicing his guitar and learning more songs. His passion for music led to his meeting others who also had a love for instruments and music. Pretty soon they formed a Western band they called the Jolly Range Riders. The wore fancy outfits made in Philadelphia at Rodeo Ben's Western Clothing

Store, where the likes of Gene Autry and Roy Rogers tailored their outfits. The band had an agent and gained some regional notoriety playing at war bond rallies and state fairs. Later, they went on to open for well-known stars including the classic "singing cowboy" Gene Autry and the Riders of the Purple Sage, many of whose members also formed a little band you might know called The Grateful Dead.

My mother, Dorothy Maude Eastwood, was a classy gal with strawberry blonde hair, a sharp wit, and very intelligent mind. Her mother was a homemaker, and her father was a carpenter and home builder. Dorothy worked as a legal secretary in Chester when she was young and single. My dad met her under a bridge in Chester one day while he was getting his shoes shined.

"Aren't you Willie Burks?" my mom had asked him that day, so the well-told story in my family went. As I heard this tale through the years, I assumed my mom knew who he was because she had seen my dad's face on some of the advertisements posted around town for his band. (Not true, I learned later.)

"Well, yes, I am Willie Burks," my dad told my mom. "What's your name?"

She told him and asked if he would like to come to church. Dad gave it some thought for several weeks before he eventually began attending. A man he befriended at church then suggested that Dad ask that "cute, single redhead over there" to go to an upcoming party. That pretty strawberry blonde redhead was the same woman he had encountered when he was getting his shoes shined. His life was about to shine in a wonderful way.

Dad gathered up his nerve and did ask my mom to the party. At the end of the evening before he took her home, they prayed together. And the rest, as the story goes, was history. Those end-of-date and end-of-day prayers continued for the next 41 years they spent as husband and wife.

In my mind, that's how the family story went, and I was satisfied. Only it wasn't ALL of the history. As hard as it is to understand, I was in my thirties before I would know about my father's past, including learning that he had a previous marriage.

Long before he moved to Chester and before he met my mom, at age 19 my dad married Mary, who was 17. Mary's father and my dad's father went to the courthouse in Appomattox, Virginia, to get their marriage license. My dad was working for the State of Virginia Road Department at the time. In about 1939 after his father-in-law moved to Sheridan, Pennsylvania, to work at a new E.J. Lavino blast furnace, Willie joined him there to learn the new trade. Willie was 20-something and wanted to advance his career, while providing a better life for his wife and young girls, Shirley and Joyce.

From there, Willie and his family moved to Chester to work in the steel mill. Between the time my dad and Mary divorced and he eventually married my mom, there was a lot of history I did not know. Fast forward to my teenage years. I saw "Aunt" Shirley and "Aunt" Joyce occasionally at our family gatherings. They were around fifteen years older than me. One day during a car ride with my dad when I was about 12, I asked him, "Who are Shirley and Joyce to me?" I don't even know why I asked that question.

"Let's wait until you are about 18 or so, and I'll answer that," my dad said.

I never gave it another thought after that day. When I would see Shirley and Joyce, it never came up in conversation. And then life happened and Dad never told me the story, until that day I was sitting in his living room.

On the whole, my family was as plain Jane as they came, I'd always believed. I had two working class parents who were firmly middle-class. They taught Sunday school every week, and I'd been their reasonably "perfect" son, at least in their eyes. That's who we were. When I learned more to the story, there was a very big moment where things started clicking into place.

My biggest takeaway was that I wasn't the ONLY one in the family who wasn't perfect after all—my father, someone I'd looked up to my whole life, was far from it as well. When he told me he'd been married at 19... similar to my being married at 20...to another gal before my mother, I was floored. When I learned he'd divorced young after they had two precious girls, again like me, I was flabbergasted. Dad corrected my thinking—Shirley and Joyce were actually my half-sisters, not my aunts as I had assumed. Joyce, Shirley, and I have since become very close in the last 35 years, and in my heart they are truly my older (insert smile) sisters whom I cherish.

I didn't know if I should feel relieved or mad that afternoon. I was relieved that I wasn't letting my parents down nearly as much as I'd feared by getting a divorce. At the same time, I could see my life's decisions had been a virtual mirror of my own father's up that point, and no one had told me. Finally, missing pieces somewhat came together and locked in place, quelling questions I'd long held but never could understand their origin.

But there were other pieces of this new section to his life story that still didn't add up for me. That's because my dad wasn't finished. There was more to tell. Much more.

When my father was married to Mary living in Chester, he had risen through the ranks at the steel mill blast furnace to become a foreman. Working in the heat amid the pressure of the job brought long and difficult days in an environment where the equipment wasn't the only thing that overheated. Steel mill towns were notoriously stressful places to live. They may call Philadelphia the City of Brotherly Love, but back then, it was often said that it was more like the City of Brotherly Shove. Men lost their tempers, and their lives, working in tight quarters with sweat and grime dripping down their bodies all day. Fights seemed to be commonplace at the mill but usually just vented some pressure that had built up during the week. The men would eventually go back to work to finish out the day. Dad wrote letters saying that many times alcohol was a contributor to the scuffles.

As a child, my dad had been picked on and bullied for his red, curly hair. Not only did he learn to defend himself, but he built up a reputation for being the "tough redhead." Over time that generated a pretty good temper in him. He was often pushed into a circle of schoolboys and riled up to fight another kid for the entertainment of other children. The next part of this story had been a bit vague up until writing this book, but newspaper archives told the truth.

EVEN OUR BEST RELATIONSHIPS ARE MESSY

"I want you to apologize for what you said," Willie had told the man. Willie glanced at his watch. It was 4:30 on February 27, 1946. The situation had been brewing since that morning when this employee accused Willie of holding up production at the steel mill in Chester.

Quitting time couldn't come too early on a day like this.

"Apologize," Willie repeated with more anger.

In a sarcastic tone the other man sneered and said, "You're just going to have to take it!"

I'm guessing Willie's mind went back to the jeering on the playground at school and the bullying he had endured, and he had enough. He was tired to the bone and looking forward to clocking out and getting home to Mary and his sweet girls where he could have some peace.

In an instant Willie reared back and punched the other man in the face with his left fist. The man fell to his knees and then over on his back, striking his head with a deafening thud on the cold pavement of the factory floor. In an instant, Willie's life was over—the worker was unconscious. Willie and others tried to revive the man, but finally an ambulance took him away to Chester Hospital where doctors discovered a skull fracture.

Soon after, Willie was arrested, escorted to jail, and charged with aggravated assault. Within a few days doctors said the man in the hospital also had a brain injury. He subsequently died, so the charges against Willie were upgraded to manslaughter. Willie was tried, found guilty, and sent to Broadmeadows Farm Prison.

My mind was reeling as I learned that my mild-mannered, gentle giant dad—my seemingly perfect father—had not only spent time in jail, but it was for manslaughter. Dad stopped the story there. It became obvious that he never really talked to me or any relatives about all the details of this life-altering event. But 35 years later, I would learn "the rest of the story," as the newscaster Paul Harvey would say. Keep reading, you will too.

Eventually my dad was released from prison and began dating my mom. Willie and Dorothy married in 1951, and I was born in 1952.

All of this happened before I was born, of course. But when I was four years old, I remember times when my father traveled far away on occasional weekends alone. These memories surfaced as I considered the timeline of my dad's story. I realized that even though he had long since left prison, he was probably traveling to check in with his parole officer and to visit Joyce and Shirley whom he loved so much.

After Dad's death, I would learn even more details of this chapter in my father's life from Bernie May, a family friend and missionary pilot who went to church with my parents and my mother's parents. Later in our sandwich journey, I will tell the rest of the details from Bernie's viewpoint. Trust me, my mind was blown a second time!

Bernie had a tremendous influence on me as a child and still does to this day. As a result of Bernie, his parents, and a prison ministry, my father became one of the strongest Christians I've ever known. Dad getting his shoes shined under a bridge, at a random time, on a random street—and my mother randomly walking by at just the right time—are almost too many things aligning to be random.

I started to unpack the coincidences, surprised by how similar my dad's situation was to my own. It wasn't as if I'd intentionally followed in my father's footsteps. It was just history repeating itself. Mary divorced Dad while he was serving time, and she retained primary custody of their two daughters. Similarly, my ex-wife would likewise retain the primary responsibility for raising our two girls after our divorce. Later on, I would meet the love of my life, Bobbie, in my mid-thirties—about the same age my dad had met and married the love of his life, my mom. Bobbie and I had one son together named Josh. Likewise, my parents had given birth to me, their only son. Knowing my dad had flaws like me was one of those, "Oh my word!" moments. It took a lot of pressure off that I'd needlessly been putting on myself.

My father died years ago, but he is still my hero BECAUSE of—not in spite of—all he went through. My father was the wisest man I'd ever known, a very strong bull of a man both physically and emotionally. Instead of shattering my image of him, the truth about his failures actually brought us closer. And it built a wonderful relationship with the women I now call sisters, Joyce and Shirley!

Truth has a way of doing that. Learning the truth also made me more CERTAIN than ever before that there was enough grace to go around for even me. If you learn nothing else from my story throughout this book, remember that. There is *more than enough grace for you*, no matter how messy your life is.

WHEN DESTINY MEETS FATE

When I was two years old, my father led us to a new community just north of Philadelphia. U.S. Steel announced it was building a modern steel plant in

Fairless Hills, which is a heck of a name for this city on the Delaware River on the Pennsylvania side across from Trenton, New Jersey. My parents bought a house for $10,300 in a master-planned community called Levittown. Their payments were $59 per month. It was one of the first subdivisions of its kind in America, where every house looked like its neighbor's with a perfectly portioned green square of lawn in front.

The steel plant employed up to 8,000 people at its height, and most of them lived in this self-contained community of schools and shopping centers where residents could find everything they needed without ever leaving the neighborhood. Everyone was middle class like me, and we felt like equals because we all went to the same schools in this manufactured picture of the American dream. It was a great place to grow up—albeit a little Stepford Wives-esque in retrospect. I lived there until my senior year of high school.

My dad was fortunate to find work after his stint in prison, although he never did go into management again. He was content to be a common laborer and held down shiftwork for the rest of his life, working 8-4, 4-12, and 12-8 shifts through the great times, as well as the labor strikes. When he had time off, or while workers were on strike, he was busy performing carpentry work on the side, painting for neighbors and even plowing for small-time farmers who could use the help. He was always working hard to make ends meet for our family. My mom left work as a legal secretary and became a homemaker when I was born. She made sure our family found a solid church to attend when we moved, and the nearest one was Calvary Baptist Church in Bristol, Pennsylvania.

When I was a teen, Dad set me up with a workbench where I could spread out a bunch of electronics parts to fiddle with. He always kept several woodworking projects going during his free time. I taught myself basic electronics and built my own contraptions using parts from old radios and televisions that he brought home to me. I would strip them of all components, meticulously cataloging each item. One by one I'd examine them to find out what made those radios and TVs tick. I could tell a resistor from a capacitor before I learned my math tables.

The music and familiar chatter of WBCB, a low-power AM station in Levittown, filled the hours I spent tinkering in my dad's workshop on weekends and after school. This little radio station broadcast a mere 1000 watts during the day and dropped to just 250 watts at night—a feat of radio engineering that fascinated me. I even called the WBCB station one night to ask the DJ how they were able to broadcast so far using what amounted to a lightbulb's worth of power.

My ninth-grade English teacher was a young bachelor and music buff who seemed to be living the dream, as far as I could tell, moonlighting as a WBCB DJ after school each day. When I peppered him with questions about his job, he just said, "Hey kid—I'd be spending all my time playing records alone at home, if I wasn't working there. So why not get paid for it?" Made sense to me. It didn't get better than that, I thought—finding something you love and getting paid for doing it. But how could you make a living in radio?

Later that year I visited a Pennsylvania Christian FM station named WCHR for my first official tour of a studio. WCHR 94.5 FM went on the air in August of 1964. I never forgot what it felt like sitting alongside the DJ, Chuck Zulker, in the booth that day. He always made a point to pronounce the "W" in their call letters as "Doubled-U." I became a regular visitor to the station after that day, happy just to observe the daily goings on.

Because we were a Christian family, I also wanted to commit my life to God when I was young. But I feared doing so would mean becoming a missionary in the wilds of Africa. I'd seen those missionaries as a child in our church—you know, the ones with open-toed sandals who live in countries you can't pronounce where people sweat a lot. I knew what I was talking about. I wanted to serve God, but I did not want to wear open-toed sandals. And I sure didn't want to sweat.

Then I got a chance to go with the missions director of our church and his family to the Caribbean island of Bonaire, which also happened to be the home of Trans World Radio. TWR is the largest Christian media organization in the world today and broadcasts

Bible teaching and music programming to almost 200 countries. I have the whitest skin of any white guy I've ever met, and I got the worst sunburn of my life while there. But I also saw something in Bonaire I'd never seen before—missionaries in radio. To coin a phrase from the 60s, they were hip. Classy. And they wore regular shoes to work.

"Holy moly," I remember thinking. It changed my whole attitude about what a missionary could be.

I spent over a week in the beautiful Caribbean and found myself in heaven—not on the beach with tourists, but inside the four walls of the radio production studios. Trans World was putting out a half-million watts using a transmitter so big that you could walk inside of it. And their recording studio rivaled any professional outfit in New York at the time. I was hooked. Somehow, someway, I was going to be in radio.

I surrendered my life to God without reservation after that trip and told him to do with it whatever he wished. It's liberating to realize that God just wants the AVAILABLE people—the ones who say to him, "Use me however you want." At the same time, those are the scariest words someone can say. There is a character in the Bible I like named Moses. Despite Moses' loud protests that he was NOT qualified for the job, God used Moses to lead the Hebrew people out of Egyptian slavery. And you know what? History proved that this unqualified guy was actually the perfect one to accomplish the task.

I could at least hope for something similar in my own life, albeit on a much more modest scale. I didn't have any particular talents at the time that God could use, but I also had nothing else on my calendar! I was available.

Relationships often fall under the category of The Sloppy Joe. A personal relationship with God is no different and has its own challenges. Our relationships with family, friends, colleagues, and business partners can and often do get complicated and a little hard to handle. While they can be incredibly fulfilling and downright enjoyable—these relationships don't often stay in their lane, and they tend to not be neat and tidy all the time. How can you have a relationship with God, someone you can't see or touch? It's not always easy, as the rest of my Sloppy Joe story will show you.

MR. WINDER PLANTS A DREAM

I graduated from Woodrow Wilson High School in 1970 with my high school diploma, as well as a certification in instrumentation from Bucks County Technical School. As part of my education, I alternated attending two weeks at the technical school with two weeks of regular high school. The tech school was ahead of its time for that era and offered classes in plumbing, electrical, data instrumentation, drafting, culinary arts, horticulture, and several other disciplines.

I am the poster child for today's public career technology centers that have sprung up all over our nation to offer young teens a hands-on education that they cannot receive within a traditional classroom. My experience as a teen is a big part of why I helped found the Tyler Innovation Pipeline (TIP) in the city where we live now. I wanted to give other students even more advanced opportunities to pursue their passion in diverse technology fields. What started as a dream among a handful of other local techies like myself who met for lunch downtown in Tyler is now a membership-based program that provides a place for innovative ideas and the tools to build those ideas. If TIP had been available to me as a kid, I think I would have tried to live there full-time.

My high school Sunday school teacher, Mr. Winder, came to class one morning talking about a trip he'd just taken to Texas. He set aside his Sunday school lesson long enough to tell us boys about a place we'd only read about in books, where cowboys ruled the Wild West and tumbleweeds rambled across everyone's yards.

"Boys, let me tell you something," he said, leaning forward in his metal folding chair. "Texas lets you drive a car when you are just 15 years of age!"

He had our attention then. Sixteen was the legal driving age in Pennsylvania, and that seemed like forever to wait for us 14-year-old boys. And then he introduced us to R.G. LeTourneau, a businessman and the president of a school he founded called LeTourneau Technical Institute somewhere in East Texas.

He explained how LeTourneau had amassed a personal fortune building gigantic earth-moving machines. I was all about that kind of thing—the big business success AND the big machines. "Mr. LeTourneau gives to the Lord 90% of his earnings," Mr. Winder added. When Mom and Dad started talking to me about attending college, Mr. Winder's story came to mind. We wrote off for some brochures from LeTourneau, and I also applied to Moody Bible Institute in Chicago. I was looking for a faith-based school with an engineering bent, and both Moody and LeTourneau fit that description.

WHERE HAVE I LANDED?

No one in my family had been to college, to my knowledge. However, there was no question I would get a degree. LeTourneau was the first one to accept me, and I hurried down there to Texas after graduation before they could change their minds. My dad couldn't take off work long enough to take me to Texas, so my parents bought me a plane ticket, packed a footlocker for me, and shipped it ahead of my arrival at the dorms. I boarded the plane in Philadelphia alone in August and for the next few hours pictured my mom's tears as we'd said goodbye.

I exited the commercial jet in Shreveport, Louisiana, and caught a smaller plane we jokingly came to refer to as Treetop Airlines. It flew over the Pineywoods to Gregg County airport in Longview, Texas, about an hour west of the Louisiana border. When I walked down the narrow staircase to the tarmac that summer day, I took a deep breath of the most foul-smelling air I'd ever breathed—a potent mixture of what reminded me of nail polish and rotten eggs. I later learned that the stench tainting the air was a fixture of that area, courtesy of nearby Eastman Chemical. The locals called it "the smell of money"!

I had never been to the South, much less Texas, in my life. I'd only seen photos of the campus where I would spend the next four years away from my family, friends, and everything familiar to me. I looked around as I walked into the airport terminal to catch a ride to campus and thought, "Where am I, and what have I done?" I could sense more Sloppy Joe sandwiches looming in my future, and it was about to get really sloppy.

TWO

The B-L-T

Why do they call this sandwich The B-L-T? Why is it never The L-T-B? Probably because everything really is better with bacon, not necessarily with lettuce or tomato! This chapter in my story is aptly named The B-L-T because I've learned that there really is an order to things going on behind the scenes, even when all you see is a series of unconnected events linked by random, embarrassing mess-ups and failures. When you build this sandwich, you start with the bacon, then the lettuce, and then the tomato in the traditional order of items. In my story, it was crucial that things happen in order. I developed a passion and then struggled in my initial pursuit of it many times. Your life may have a different order to events, but there IS an order. Even when you don't think your life makes sense as you traipse from one brilliant disappointment to another, you're building a B-L-T. As a young man in my early twenties, the turn of events had to happen that way, at that exact time, so that I could learn some foundational truths about who God is and if he could really be trusted with something as precious as our plans for our future.

THREE STEPS FORWARD, TWO STEPS BACK

In high school, I'd enjoyed a busy social life. However, I intended to knuckle down after went to college. I would focus on my studies and continue my growing love affair with radio and broadcasting. I didn't necessarily keep those first two intentions in college, but I fell head over heels for radio.

As a freshman at LeTourneau, I headed over to the campus radio station one day to look for a job. It was a very small operation, really more of a hobby, and they happened to have some openings for on-air shifts. Frankly, they were open to anyone who had a pulse. I was hired on the spot, but I cautioned my mom not to be too impressed. I told her I was merely a warm body who could fill a time slot and spin discs. But the size of the job didn't matter to me, because I now had a chance to hone my craft. I know only five people likely listened to my show, but I created a binder full of stories and banter to use between records.

In my free time, I listened to the Longview radio station KFRO, a local icon that had been broadcasting AM programming since the heyday of radio in the 1930s. Radio personality Paul Harvey was once one of the most recognized voices in America, and KFRO's claim to fame was that Harvey had broadcast his daily program from their studio when he visited Longview on a tour of Texas. One day the DJ at KFRO mentioned on air that they needed someone to call basketball games on the radio for the LeTourneau Yellow Jackets. I applied in person.

I walked into KFRO and was instantly transported in time to something resembling a back room at the Sahara in Vegas, circa 1950. There was a sleek black piano next to a single microphone, and the place reeked of cigarette smoke. The walls were coated in rivulets of nicotine stains, including crude, yellowed egg crates lining the broadcast studio for cheap soundproofing. I talked with the station manager for a while, left a demo tape from my campus radio broadcast, and hoped for the best.

I got the job at KFRO, but there was a problem. I am not a sports guy. Translation: I knew nothing about basketball. Calling my first basketball game on air was horrid and went something like: *"There's someone running down on the left side. He shoots. He misses. Oh, nuts. Well, now they're going back the other way."* It was THAT bad.

I immediately set about finding a guy who could give me pointers on the finer elements of the sport. I found someone who was a friend of a friend, and he and I traveled to games together so I could pick up the proper terminology and learn the banter. Although calling games for KFRO wasn't much in the way of opportunity, I was building confidence, as well as experience on the air. This gig eventually led to hosting a regular Sunday morning on-air program at KFRO that I enjoyed and, thankfully, did not involve athletics.

STUCK NEEDLES AND OTHER DISASTERS

My Sunday shift was from six in the morning until noon and included broadcasting various pre-recorded church services. I worked alone in the tiny studio, and the station owner trusted me with a set of keys to let myself in every Sunday. These 30-minute religious programs arrived in the KFRO mailbox on oversized, long-playing vinyl records. Once I dropped the needle on a recording, I had nothing to do for exactly half an hour. One morning I calculated that I had just enough time to skip out of the studio and walk down the street to a local landmark hotel for a cup of coffee and make it back by the end of the program with a few minutes to spare. At seven on the dot, I began playing that week's selection from the "Salvation Army Program of the Air," locked up the studio, and left.

I made my way downtown and strolled through the doors of the hotel lobby, a nostalgic locale from the Thirties with the distinction of being the second hotel acquired by Conrad Hilton for his new family hotel chain. I ordered my coffee and quickly made my way back to the studio after stealing away for my little adventure.

When I unlocked the downstairs door, I knew immediately something was wrong. There were two phone lines that rang into the studio—one for listeners and a hotline reserved for the station owner. Both were ringing. Over their incessant shrill, I also heard a booming voice that drained my face of any color, leaving me lightheaded and sick to my stomach.

"Aaaaand you're going to hell...Aaaaand you're going to hell..." The needle was stuck in a groove on the record, and the preacher's voice was repeating this phrase over and over live on the air!

I ran up the stairs to the second-story studio, dashed headlong toward the control board, and lunged for the needle, nudging it forward with one hand and scooping up the receiver on the hotline with the other. I received an earful from the owner about my mistake, but I managed to apologize profusely enough to keep my job!

Also in the category of being bold and stupid but not dead, I remember getting a wild hair one day to see if I could hook up a telephone in my college dorm room. After all, the kid at the end of Tyler Hall had one. He was a tough, outdoorsy guy from North Carolina we fondly nicknamed Frankie-poo. These days he goes by Franklin Graham, son of the late evangelist Billy Graham.

No, I didn't ask permission to install a phone; nor did I

have a clue about what I was doing. But I thought I could figure it out the day I noticed a bundle of multicolored wires behind a wall plate near my desk. Curious, I then wrangled a telephone handset with a battery and studied the wiring. Next, I dug into the bundle of wires on the wall, connecting the phone over and over until I got a dial tone! Eureka!

At home, I had taken apart our rotary dial phone more than once, much to my mother's dismay. I quickly learned that spinning the dial rapidly broke the circuit and made the circuit again while dialing numbers. When you dialed a "3," for example, it would pop the circuit three times. In my dorm room, I practiced quickly making and breaking the connection manually to dial phone numbers. The first thing I learned the hard way, after accidentally dialing some extension in the administration building, was that I had to dial "9" to get an outside line. Note to self.

When I got up the guts, I then dialed a "9," carefully timing it and counting while waiting for another dial tone. Then I proceeded to make and break the circuit, dialing the 11 numbers for my parents back in Levittown. Sure enough, it worked! I never told my parents or anyone else until now (don't tell anyone) how I hacked the college phone system! Later in life, I felt guilty about the long-distance charges and sent a check to the university, citing "no particular reason."

That hack led to another daring move that could *never* happen today. Feeling the joy of my newly-learned telephony skills, on a whim I drove to downtown Longview about 9:00pm and found the Bell Telephone Central Office (CO) building. A side door happened to be propped open, begging me to go inside. So I did. I wandered into a noisy room with the clatter of relays and switches sending calls all over the city and connecting circuits to all parts of the world. My eyes followed a 36-inch bundle of tiny wires, and I imagined my phone call to my parents traveling those very wires. Fascinating.

I saw one employee, but he didn't notice me for about two full minutes. When he did turn around, he was so startled that he nearly fell. He started yelling at me to get out and asking how I got in, between a few other obscenities all strung together. When he took a breath, I quickly told him I was an engineering student from LeTourneau with a "telephony background" (I'm a hacker after all). I just wanted to see the CO and learn how it works, I explained. He calmed down at that point, and 90 minutes later I left way smarter than when I walked in. And I was still alive!

Looking back, I see that I was learning the importance of maintaining curiosity and persistence throughout life whenever possible. My deep curiosity as a teen about how things worked left my mother shaking her head, which led to "hacking," which led to boldly going into a building in downtown Longview where no 20-something should have gone. But, all of it also eventually landed me a job. See what I mean about The B-L-T? Life has order and meaning. You're not just existing day to day. As a person of faith, I find purpose in everything that comes my way, and I believe it is all working together for my good.

IF IT WEREN'T FOR BAD LUCK...

One day, two friends of mine in the electrical engineering department at school heard someone was building a gospel radio station in the nearby city of Gilmer. We drove over just as the workers poured the concrete block for the base of the radio tower. It's true—being in the right place at the right time leads to opportunities. We introduced ourselves to the station owners, who issued us an invitation that afternoon to help build the rest of the station from the ground up. We were eager, hungry, and cheap!

Even though we had zero experience in this line of work, the three of us engineers got to work figuring it out step-by-step. We even took an old transmitter that had been in storage for years and performed a Frankenstein-like work on it that brought it back to life. We only blew it up twice. I strung cable and wired the studio myself in the final steps to get KHYM-AM on the air, something I would repeat on a much larger scale in my career years later on a number of occasions.

I became the program director for this fledgling 5000-watt clear channel station that broadcast its signal from a sleepy town of just a few thousand people. Many times a week I made the two-lane highway drive from Longview to Gilmer to play gospel hits until my shift ended at 5:30 in the afternoon, before racing back to Longview to pick up an evening shift as a rock-and-roll DJ at KFRO.

The host before me in the KFRO studio followed a strict routine, walking out of the studio promptly at six at the start of the news. If I didn't make it into the studio by 6:05, the end of the network news segment, it was dead air. Night after night I burst into the studio at the last minute, threw on my headphones, and signed on as Woody Savage playing pre-pubescent teenie-bopper bubble gum rock until 10:30. I'd chosen a pseudonym because it helped me make the mental shift from playing KHYM's *The Old Rugged Cross* "with your host Phil Burks" to lining up hours of America's Top 40 on KFRO. The inspiration for my name was an old movie with a character named Paul Savage and Eastwood, my middle name.

I often joked on air with my listeners how, once again, I didn't have time to eat dinner before my shift began. One night the doorbell rang at the studio, and I went downstairs to find a young girl standing outside, holding a sack of food.

"Mr. Savage, my mom says you didn't get supper," she began. "So she made you a steak dinner." And she handed me the sack.

I smiled and thanked her. Woody Savage and hundreds of other local disc jockeys across America were household names to families who let us into their lives each evening. That was something I liked about radio—it had the ability to reach out across the miles and entertain people no matter where they were.

MAKING MY MOVE INTO TELEVISION

One day I heard about a nationwide radio contest for the "Best Gospel DJ in the United States." Listeners could nominate their favorite DJ and propel some lucky winner to the most coveted spot in gospel radio. I pushed the contest on the air at KHYM every chance I got and shamelessly prodded listeners to give me their vote. This was back in the day when nominations were sent off by regular mail, not tweeted or texted, so I endured an agonizing wait for the results. I basically loaded the ballot box, but to my delight I actually won! Given our market size, this was a big deal for East Texas. The station owner sent out a press release announcing the win. Then a local ABC television affiliate in Tyler picked up the story and sent a crew on the 45-minute drive to Gilmer to interview me at the tiny station inside a double-wide mobile home, nestled in the middle of a field next to a cemetery.

After the interview, the reporter made the mistake of casually inviting me to Tyler to visit the Channel 7 KLTV studio anytime, which I made sure I did on a regular basis. I am nothing if not determined (remember me strolling into the telephone office?). I made excuses to drop by so often that one day Michael Brown, the lead anchor at the time, pointed at me and asked me to fetch him something he needed while he was on a commercial break.

"Thanks," he said when I returned with the item. Then he eyed me suspiciously. "Do you work here?" he asked.

"No," I said truthfully, "but I'd like to." Cue big TV smile.

Michael scowled back and told me to send in my resumé, and several months later I got a job at KLTV as the Longview-based news correspondent. I really don't like the word "luck." But for simplicity, I'm going to use it here. I consider this stroke of luck the "bacon" in my B-L-T. Bacon is the good stuff! Maybe you're feeling like a flop because you just have the tomato and lettuce and you're waiting on some good stuff to happen in your life. It's on its way. Wait and see. This job really added something unique to my life. I wouldn't trade the experience because I finally fulfilled a dream I had way back in high school.

In addition to my engineering courses and radio work, I took jobs in the snack bar and dish room in the college cafeteria to earn extra money. I struggled in my coursework but pressed on. My parents were paying for my education (nothing extra), and I did not want to let them down.

Outside of work, I didn't have much spare time for anything but studying. I did well with my academic goals my first year off at school—not so good my second year or thereafter. Everyone on our dormitory floor called ourselves Flooders, a name bestowed by the engineering geniuses residing on the third floor of our dorm in 1968 who built a swimming pool in a shower that didn't work out so well. Neither Franklin nor I had anything to do with the flood, but we did participate in our share of shenanigans. One of us even got kicked out of school, and I'm not saying which one.

I met Lee during my second year of school, and we married in 1972 while we were both full-time students. I was busier than ever, holding down jobs and starting a new family. In my work as the Longview TV correspondent, I'd film a story of interest in Longview and drive it over to the Tyler studio every day. With help from Barry Hanson, a KLTV celebrity, I learned to shoot and develop 16mm film, produce stories, and put them on air.

John (Big Santa) Bass was the sports reporter for KLTV, and I accompanied him many weekends throughout the football season to cover high school games. One Friday night he was scheduled to interview a promising young football player in Tyler who had broken several records. I got to Rose Stadium early to set up at the field house to the left of the stadium. I mistakenly turned on a set of high-power camera lights and was promptly chewed out by a referee for nearly blinding the players and coaches who were trying to finish the game.

John pulled the player aside after the final score,

and I started the camera rolling. He did a great job interviewing the kid, and I went back to the station to process the film. When I opened up the camera in the darkroom, my heart sunk. I had made a HUGE mistake. Somehow I'd incorrectly threaded the roll and had nothing on the film. John not only missed his report that night but also missed the archive-worthy opportunity to capture an early interview with future Heisman trophy winner and Hall of Famer Earl Campbell, nicknamed the "Tyler Rose."

John forgave me eventually, but there is always drama in a newsroom—a truism I continued to discover when I eventually worked my way up to becoming the weekend news anchor for KLTV. I reported on the good, bad, and the ugly that every community has. I'm a sensitive guy, so it was the stories about death and violence that stuck with me long after the newscast was over. I once came across a terrible head-on wreck while driving back home to Longview. I had to call it in to the sheriff's department since I was the first person on the scene. The wheels of an overturned vehicle were still spinning, and the bright headlights of a van parted the darkness with an eerie beam of white light shining through steam escaping from the hot engine. In my mind, I can still see one of the girls in the carload of cheerleaders sobbing and choking on a mouthful of blood. All her teeth were missing. To this day, I've never been able to get that "story" out of my mind. In the future, I would have a hand in sending help to the scene of accidents like that all over the country. But I didn't know that then. The technology didn't even exist.

Inside the studio, television reporters read whatever stories came off the teletype machine, instead of using a teleprompter like they do today. "Rip and read" reporting was the name of the game, and most of our 30-minute news programs were punctuated by a series of video clips to accompany each story.

I began every broadcast at KLTV the same way. "Good evening, everyone. I'm Phil Burks, and this is the news..." and then I'd tease the first story, followed by the corresponding prepared video clip. One night I teased the first story but heard the director in my earpiece tell me to go to the next story.

"Well, folks, we seem to have a problem..." I explained, moving swiftly to the next story on the page only to find out through my earpiece that something was seriously wrong. The giant machine called a TCR had eaten the videocassettes containing ALL my film clips for the entire newscast. I could barely focus while my right ear filled with cursing, heavy breathing, and what sounded like a baseball bat being taken to the TCR as the frustrated news director banged on the machine in an attempt to make it cough up the goods.

A skeleton crew usually produces weekend newscasts in smaller markets, and ours was no exception. It was up to the handful of us to come up with a solution on live television—and fast! Looking steadily into the camera, I reached behind me and slyly turned off my microphone. Then I performed my best ventriloquist smile and whispered to the weather girl, "Get me some fill copy. Quick!"

She ran full speed to rip a dozen more stories off the teletype machine. Out of the corner of my eye, I saw her dive for the tile floor and crawl under the news desk to hand them to me off-camera.

By the time I'd read 28 minutes of fill copy to pad the newscast, I'd sweated through my shirt. The problem with the video feed was, of course, fixed just in time for the closing commercial! I drove home that night exhausted.

Then there was the night when the cameraman had not locked the main camera in place before walking 10 feet away to aim another camera. I was on-air and could see in the monitor the shot of my head slowly falling off screen. I had to think fast. I grabbed my 20 pages of news copy, planted my feet on the floor, and pedaled the wheels of my chair to track with the rogue camera—rolling to the other side of the news desk to stay in the shot. It worked! Weekends in the TV industry were always memorable.

I had to fail early on in my radio and television days before I could succeed in something else. I had to apply for jobs I was not qualified to do—and then I had to learn the lingo on the fly. I had to learn responsibility at the radio station after my fiasco with the broken record. I had to be creative when things went wrong at the TV station.

Learning to recognize what you're good at and matching that with the opportunities available to you is an important key to success. That's what I mean by looking at the events and circumstances in your life and trying to see order from the chaos. You're building the most awesome B-L-T—Bacon Lettuce Tomato sandwich—from the raw events in your life, and it's going to be amazing when it's finished. But first it may feel more like a L-B-T or a T-B-L when you're trying to assemble a life, a career, a family, and a purpose for yourself. It often takes trial and error and finding out what you DON'T enjoy doing before you can zero in on the particular talents you DO have and then plan how you can make a living at them. Sometimes a closed door can tell you more about what you're supposed to be doing than an open door ever could.

I'M (NOT) GOING TO BE A MISSIONARY

I graduated from LeTourneau in 1974.5 after having spent an extra semester for good measure to earn my Electrical Engineering Technology degree. My degree allows me to legally tell you where and how hard to kick something to make it work! I then applied to be a missionary with the Moody Broadcasting Network, an iconic name in Christian radio and something that would be a dream come true for me. I thought the job at Moody would be a perfect and natural fit with what God seemed to be leading me to do, given my passion and experience.

The leaders at the network seemed to agree when they saw my application, and Moody flew me out to Spokane, Washington, for an interview. I nailed the interview, returned home, and began mentally preparing Lee for our drive out to Washington State where I would start work. I would finally be fulfilling the promise I'd made God earlier about serving him, and I felt darn good about that. Shortly afterward, Moody contacted me by letter to thank me for my time. But, they wrote, I was not their guy. What? I mean, WHAT?

I took this news hard and honestly thought my world had collapsed. Not their guy? "Hey, God," I wanted to say. "I surrendered to be your full-time missionary, remember? I'm THAT guy. What's going on?"

I'd led a pretty charmed life up to that point. My parents were still together when many kids' parents, including my best friend's, had split up. I'd been given a lot of responsibility in the youth group and at church throughout high school. Pretty much anything I'd tried, I'd been successful in doing. I have loved the performing arts since I was a kid and even landed the coveted starring role in Camelot as King Arthur my senior year. I'd graduated from my university of choice and was on the cusp of starting my future serving the Lord. And now Moody was saying I wasn't the right man? King Arthur? Hello?

I had the extra stress of wanting to get a job and

support my new family. The more I thought about it, the angrier I was with God for messing things up. Remember, a relationship with God is sometimes messy. See Chapter 1. This time in my life marked a tailspin into an extended period of doubt and confusion that lasted longer than it should have. I finally stopped complaining and shut up long enough to listen to what God was really saying to me all along. And what he had to say surprised me.

As far as missions was concerned, God was NOT leading me to a hard-to-pronounce country or even a well-known radio network to serve him full-time after all. God was NOT calling me to *go*...but to *send*. I distinctly sensed he was leading me to be a businessman, who was ALSO a believer in Jesus' love and made it possible for others to go into missions. I finally understood that I didn't have to go to the mission field myself—I just needed to get busy working so I could be a conduit and support others who went in my place.

I had been trying so hard to make a T-L-B out of my life, when the right order all along was B-L-T. I had to be rejected and fall into a funk before I could see what I was really supposed to do after graduation. This was the first time I got my B-L-T in the right order.

Granted, this insight about being a successful businessman came to me when I was a young twenty-something with no other job prospects. Was I worried about funding others' calling to missions and ministry when I could barely put two nickels together? Heavens, yes. But I was relieved to realize that at least I was still in the game—God had a plan for me. It wasn't that I had failed right out of the gate after graduation. I just hadn't found my niche.

I eventually emerged from my pit determined to find and focus on a new career. R.G. LeTourneau became my inspiration once again. His inventions and patents were ahead of his time, and his innovative machines and equipment were used throughout the world. During World War II, LeTourneau was the unsung hero supplying the Allies with three-fourths of their earth-moving equipment used in the war. He held over 300 patents in his lifetime and became a generous philanthropist who supported many people-helping causes he believed in.

"If you're calling me to be a businessman, then make me the best businessman you can make out of a guy like me," I remember saying out loud to God one day. And then I took it one step further and added, almost like an aside, "...and make me a millionaire for you."

I wonder sometimes if we really know what we're asking when we come up with some of the ideas we have for our lives. I sensed I had a huge calling early on, but I wasn't sure what to do with that feeling. I didn't have aspirations for greatness. Honestly. God took what I said in this prayer more seriously than I did and drug me along in the process. All that follows in my story is what Jesus said in Luke 16:10, "Whoever can be trusted with very little can also be trusted with much..." All I did along the way was ask him to trust me with a little responsibility and then test me with a little bit more.

We like it when someone entrusts us with the good stuff like pay raises, promotions, and opportunities. But the testing component that always comes along with increased responsibility? We don't like that so much. If this dream of mine that I had in my twenties came true one day, I had the distinct sense that it would not be a cake walk. I was right because building a business would test me to the core—my character, my convictions, my bank account, and virtually all my relationships—in more ways than one. But what if it really did happen? Time would tell, and it would have to come in the right B-L-T order.

THREE

The East Texas Grinder

I n addition to my full-time job at Channel 7, I discovered I also had some natural salesmanship ability. I put it to work making a decent living at the mom-and-pop business telephone system installation and service shop called CSC Telephones in Longview. They hired me because I had "telephone experience"—which I never publicly connected to my hacking background!

Until 1968, you could use nothing but a Bell Telephone-provided phone set or PBX on the Bell phone lines. On June 22, 1968, the FCC ruled that Thomas Carter (Carterfone) of Gun Barrel City, Texas, had the legal right to connect his invention to the lines to allow ham operators to patch calls around the globe. Mr.

Carter was a hacker, too! That ruling opened up new industries of selling and installing non-Bell phones to businesses, including answering machines, modems, fax machines, etc. Interconnect telephone companies like CSC Telephones got in on the game and started popping up all over America.

One of my first CSC phone installs was in Marshall, Texas, for a very successful businessman named Piggy. His rapidly growing insurance business had taken over the building next door to his office downtown. All the older brick buildings lining the town square shared a common wall and attic space. Piggy had already knocked out part of the shared wall to form a doorway between the two offices. He'd also carved out a two-foot round section of the wall inside the attic so my supervisor, Tom, and I could run wiring for his phones inside the new space.

When we arrived, Tom told me to go up in the attic, squeeze through the hole Piggy had made, and lay the phone cable next door.

Dragging a big phone cable tied to my waist, I climbed a rickety ladder and carefully crawled around old gas lines and electrical wiring in the dusty attic. After I positioned the line in the right place and started making my way back through the small opening in the wall, I became stuck. Like, really stuck. I could not go forward or backward.

Tom hollered up at me just about that time. "I'm going to lunch, ok?"

"You've got to be kidding me," I thought to myself, unable to catch my breath long enough to reply.

"Hey...I'm...stuck!" I managed to breathe out in the loudest voice I could muster, which wasn't that loud considering my chest was wedged in tight, not to mention all the air handler noise rambling around in the open space.

"See you in a bit," Tom called cheerily, oblivious to my predicament. I heard the door open and close behind him.

For the next hour, I tried everything to free myself, to no avail. I finally gave up and decided to wait it out until Tom finished lunch. It was an eternity before he returned and discovered me in the attic, still stuck.

"Whatcha doin' up there, Phil?" Tom asked, firing a beam from his flashlight into the attic. My trapped torso resembled an African animal wall mount with my arms pinned behind me.

"Tom," I said, *"I'm stuck!"* I was exhausted and frustrated from trying to wriggle myself out of this mess. Tom eventually freed me with a crowbar, minus a few more bricks in the wall, and I lived to tell the tale.

Sometimes in life we all get stuck like that. We cannot move forward or backward, try as we might, and it starts to look as if we're out of options. Failure will do that to you. You'll get stuck, and the future will look bleak. You'll even be tempted to give up on your dreams altogether. I'm convinced that all the negative σκύβαλα ("skybala," in Greek...look it up) that happens is just the building materials for a great story you'll have the chance to tell other people later. My wife, Bobbie, calls it the fertilizer that grows a better life.

This is all part of the polishing process—you mess up, learn something about yourself, take a few more steps backward, and then you push forward. Even if the net result on a certain day is still backward, I try to finish every day taking one small step forward. Do that, and you'll remind yourself that you can't afford to give up. Not so soon. The tiniest step of progress is enough to remember that you really CAN do this stuff—whatever it is you're called to do in life—and that, most important, you may fail sometimes but YOU are not a failure. Just keep pushing, and I promise you'll get unstuck. Remember, someone who is in motion is easier for God to direct than someone who just remains stuck.

THE GRINDER

If I thought about it in sandwich terms, I'd call my late twenties and thirties The East Texas Grinder. I was working night and day trying to carve out a career and be successful. It required long hours and overtime to get anything done. I also inadvertently put my family through The Grinder because of the stress I carried. You folks nearing retirement in your sixties remember those days, don't you? You were the new kid on the block, and you had to think on your feet and work hard every day just to make it.

I love meeting with young people who are in high school or college to talk about their future careers, especially those who feel stuck. Everything ahead is so daunting that they feel paralyzed. They're looking at an uncertain future and coming up empty. So they want to talk to someone who knows the ropes. Sometimes they've heard about my company Genesis because of our role in the community. And sometimes they might be familiar with one of my other interests, such as Tyler Innovation Pipeline. Or maybe they're into drones and have heard about how we're revolutionizing public safety using FIRST iZ® drone technology.

A lot of our conversations follow the same pattern. I give them a quick tour of the Genesis offices and operations, followed by the elevator speech of how Genesis grew from a single DOS-based billing software product I wrote in my bedroom to where we are today with over 30 Windows- and browser-based software products for Motorola and clients from Canada to Saudi Arabia, an office in London, and close affiliates in Melbourne and Mexico City.

We sit in my office after the tour, and they often ask the same thing. "How did you DO all this?" I wonder that myself sometimes. But I make a point to immediately burst their bubble by telling them it wasn't easy and that I messed up plenty of times. And when this book is published, I'm going to give each one of them a copy and dog-ear all the pages that record my favorite missteps along the way.

"All you see is the duck above the water," I tell them, "not the furious paddling going on below the surface." I am quick to talk about the hard work and some of the ups and downs along the way to get where I am today. One of the ups was the conversation I had with a Motorola representative while working for Channel 7.

MOTOROLA ENTERS THE PICTURE

My nickname at Channel 7 was Porcupine because I drove a car with antennas sticking out all over the hood. I had an early version mobile phone loaded in my trunk. Whenever I made a call, it sucked so much power from the car battery that the lights on my dash would dim. When I wasn't on the road, I was constantly in and out of my local radio shop repairing various equipment. A Motorola sales guy also frequented that store in his line of work, and we became friends.

"You ought to come work for me," my friend told me one day when we were shooting the breeze at the shop counter.

I felt rich at the time, making a whopping $130 a week at Channel 7, plus my business phone system installation work. When the man told me what I could make working for Motorola, I no longer felt rich! I changed jobs immediately and joined the Motorola sales team. I left my old job with the telephone company and

Channel 7 on very good terms, a professional practice that would serve me well in the future. Nothing is by accident. Business relationships and opportunities often come full circle over time throughout the life cycle of your career. Keep your bridge burning to a minimum—you never know when you might need to cross back over one.

At Motorola, I sold two-way radios and radio tower space to a bunch of companies: electrical companies, plumbing companies, HVAC companies, oilfield companies, delivery companies, and anyone who needed to talk with a fleet of trucks spread out over the hills of East Texas. Not unlike eating an East Texas Grinder sandwich, I'd have to break down the cost of a radio system into bite-sized math for my customers. If the total bill were $100,000 for radios, and the company had 20 trucks, I would show them that the cost, in one year, would be about $15/day per truck.

Then I'd ask if they felt they could save more than $15 each day in fuel, time, and customer loyalty. Not a hard sell when you break it down! I came to realize that if you had to talk someone into buying (like the classic used car salesman), then you're doing it wrong. I talked to potential customers as if they were asking my advice. I simply guided the conversation and answered their questions.

Being the newbie in corporate America, I was impressed that a big corporation like Motorola handed out quarterly and annual sales awards for doing something that came naturally to me. I enjoyed being out in the field meeting people and providing useful services for them. I built great memories during this time and acquired a collection of acrylic and paper sales trophies from Motorola, not to mention a pretty cool diamond-encrusted ring engraved with 1978 on it that I rediscover from time to time in the back of my desk drawer when I'm looking for something else.

I also developed an extensive customer base and tried to deliver more than expected on every contract. There are always impediments to selling, and I vigilantly looked for ways to remove these and close each deal quicker to increase my efficiency. The issue often came down to the fact that I was selling big ticket items. Completing the sale of a huge tower for a single individual or company required many steps, including a long approval process with the FAA, which slowed the sales cycle significantly. Something had to give.

NECESSITY – THE MOTHER OF INVENTION

One day I talked about an idea to remedy this lag time with a contractor named Anthony who was building some of Motorola's towers. I asked him if he could build a single tower that I could then rent to several customers to host their radio systems, instead of building one tower per customer. I learned from Anthony that this was not a novel idea that I'd come up with. It was already being done in other markets.

Renting tower space in those larger markets was based on community repeaters. A repeater is a transmitter that intercepts a signal from a mobile radio. It then repeats the signal at a much higher power from the top of a tall tower, broadcasting it over a much greater distance. The secret sauce to radios communicating with each other over a long distance is a combination of lots of power and a tall tower—the taller, the better. This formula of power plus distance is a big deal in communications. It was a great day when those of us in the industry realized we could transmit a signal 40-50 miles off one repeater antenna positioned at the top of a tower, versus a range of just 15-25 miles with a conventional radio-to-radio system.

Better still, several companies could share a single community repeater on one tower. It functioned like a party line from the early days of telephones where several houses in a neighborhood might share one telephone line. One family could talk on the line at a time, and it was the neighborhood gossip's job to pick up the line and listen in! Likewise, in our situation several companies would share a tower, but only one company could talk at a time. The likelihood that 10 companies would be needing to talk at the very same time was reasonably low.

In a few years, a newer technology called "trunking" would eventually explode in popularity, change the industry entirely, and increase the need for towers. If you're Gen Y or younger, imagine this. There was a day when we used to pick up a phone to make a call and wait to hear a dial tone. The super brainy people who figure out stuff like this also ran algorithms to determine how many dial tones a phone company had to make available to cities to process all the calls going through at any one time. For example, a town with a population of 50,000 didn't need to provide 50,000 individual dial tones, only let's say about 10,000. The same kind of thinking went into trunking systems, a late 70s brainchild. In case you'd like to take a deeper dive, look up Erlang Calculation, specifically Erlang C. The math is fascinating.

It's the same methodology many banks use where there's one line and many tellers. The line goes much faster because you're using the existing resources to a maximum. Grocery stores are the opposite. They have a line for every cashier, which is the most inefficient way of processing people.

During pre-cellphone days, businesses like Joe's Plumbing and Bob's Air Conditioners used push-to-talk radios to communicate between the main office and their technicians' truck radios out in the field. Trunking, however, utilized a computer to work the odds and allow several businesses to share multiple channels on the same tower. The tower relayed the signal between all the trucks, based on what channels happened to be available at that exact moment.

A little history here. Imagine Joe the plumber having

to build his own radio tower just to talk with his wife running the main office back in town. It would cost too much money and be extremely inefficient. But that is the way we USED to sell radios for individual companies. Renting airtime from Motorola on one of my radio towers made more sense. Joe's wife could push a button on an inexpensive base station at her office, which my tower repeated to Joe's push-to-talk-radio in his truck so she could tell him to stop by Old Lady Murphy's house to check on her sink. She could then push the button again to dispatch another plumber to another job. As soon as she was done talking, that channel could be automatically used by Bob the air conditioner tech and so on.

But at this stage in my career, trunking had not yet evolved, and these community repeaters were the up-and-coming venture with Motorola. I saw it as a valuable opportunity for smaller customers with tighter budgets. They would benefit from having their radio system on a community repeater so that they would not have to fork over cash for their own individual towers. Building just one tower for everyone to share would also speed up the sales process, and my customers would be in business faster.

LET'S BUILD A TOWER – AND OTHER BRIGHT IDEAS

"Where would you ideally want to build a tower like that?" I asked Anthony one day.

He explained that he'd had his eye on East Mountain,

located north of Longview and south of Gilmer, my old stomping grounds in East Texas. You have to understand that mountains in Texas are really just big hills, but East Mountain got its name from being one of the tallest viewpoints around for miles.

Anthony and I ran the numbers, and he made plans to secure the land on East Mountain for an 800-foot tower, a giant structure normally only seen in major markets like Dallas or San Antonio. I felt a personal responsibility for this project to make sure it came together smoothly for my customers, and I felt extremely pressured to get it right. So I was on site for most of the tower construction. I tried devouring The Grinder at this time in my life and career—but sometimes this Failure Sandwich felt as if it were devouring me instead! I was hardly home and when I was home, I was thinking about work. Without my seeing it, I was slowing losing my family.

The tower construction was a comedy of errors from the start. When it was time to dig the foundation and pour the concrete, it rained in the middle of the curing process. Did you know concrete can float in water? I didn't. But that's exactly what happened. When Anthony stacked the first 100 feet of tower on the wobbly foundation, I worried we'd built the Leaning Tower of Pisa. Anthony didn't sweat it. He just fixed it with some strategically-placed welding and wedges and a quick tug on the top of an unbolted section of the tower!

I had many customers already lined up to get on this

thing, and there was no time to waste, so I jumped in to help wherever I could. Anthony and I made adjustments on the fly, tackling items on the tedious checklist of requirements issued by the FAA. Almost by accident, at the last minute we found out about a new FAA rule change that applied to towers over 500 feet. The FAA required strobe lights, instead of the usual flashing red lights on taller towers.

I was the closest thing to anyone technically-minded between the two of us, so I volunteered to study up on how to wire the tower for electricity and install the strobes. Once again, I had no clue what I was doing—but I was young and eager to learn. I was the only Motorola sales guy I knew running conduit and hanging by a harness 600 feet in the air in his free time! But I had companies waiting on this tower, and I was determined to get this baby up one way or another.

In the meantime, a man running the local country music station KYKX-FM heard about what was going on at East Mountain. His vision was to be the only station broadcasting George Strait and Tanya Tucker using the strongest 100,000-watt signal from the tallest tower in East Texas. So we cut a deal with him. Anthony worked out a way to add 60 more feet of tower above our platform so KYKX could stick their antenna on the very tip top and secure their bragging rights.

Normally in East Texas, the two-way radio repeater antennas would be at the top of the tower and the repeater transmitter at the bottom. The two were linked by a long pipe called a coaxial line. This works, but it wastes a lot of power pushing the signal from the bottom all the way up the chain to the top of the tower. In major markets, however, they did it a different way. They maximized power by designing the repeater to instead rest on a platform at the crown of the tower adjacent to the antenna. That way, instead of 600 feet of coax sucking up a lot of your power, you might only have four feet.

That hadn't been tried before in East Texas, so Anthony hired a welder and built a jig in his backyard. He designed a platform for the top of our tower to link the repeater and the antenna with a short, four-foot piece of coax, resulting in no loss of power and a range of almost 60 miles!

What wasn't so easy was figuring out how to hoist our repeater from the ground to a platform located 800 feet up in the sky. I was running out of time, and the conventional tower elevator was one of the last things on Anthony's list to complete. The winch line was in, but the winching motor mechanism was not. Anthony came up with another creative solution and told me to meet him at the tower the next afternoon so we could wrap the job, and I could get my customers talking.

"Give me a hint, Anthony. How are we going to get the repeater up there?" I asked. He told me to just meet him there and promised he'd figure it out.

When I arrived the next day, the repeater was already

loaded inside the elevator.

"How are we going to ride inside with it?" I asked. I shouldn't have asked.

"We're not riding inside. There's no room. We'll stand on top," came the answer. "In case there's a problem, we can just jump off and grab hold of the tower."

That's when I noticed his pick-up truck idling a few feet away with the winching cable attached to the front bumper. One of his tower crew was sitting inside the cab, smiling and waving to me.

I waved back.

"That's John," Anthony explained as we gingerly climbed on top of the steel elevator. At Anthony's signal, John put the truck in reverse to back down the hill, dropped the pedal on the gas, and off we went!

As the surrounding pine branches grew smaller and smaller beneath us, I shouted at Anthony over the clickety clack of the moving cable, "How is John going to know when to stop us?"

That's when Anthony pulled a steel starter pistol out of this pocket and said, "I'll just fire this."

I nodded. This, I reminded myself, was Texas.

As we neared the top, Anthony fired the pistol and John hit the brakes. We bounced up and down precariously on the cable for a few seconds before it settled down. However, we had stopped about six inches short of the platform.

"Six more inches!" Anthony yelled down to John and

waved him backwards.

Six inches and three hours later, we positioned the repeater on the platform, wired it, and turned on the power. I had brought a radio with me to test the signal. It worked! It was beautiful. Our customers used it for the first time that day.

Shortly afterward, I was basking in the glow of accolades from happy customers who were able to communicate all over East Texas. But some of them reported hearing some background noise—and not the typical buzz or whiz you might expect. No, this noise was something that they all swore sounded like country music. When they said that, I knew exactly what was happening. The 100,000-watt signal from the FM antenna for KYKX located just 20 feet above the repeater was inadvertently bleeding country music hits into the electronics. I spent the next month trying everything to fix it before finally removing the doors of the repeater's weatherproof casing and throwing a black trash bag over it. Problem solved, until we could devise a proper solution.

The real problem that proved more vexing stemmed from the strobe lights, which refused to cycle through their twilight, nighttime pulse, and daylight settings and instead remained stuck on the blinding daylight setting 24 hours a day! When surrounding farmers started complaining that their cows had stopped producing milk and several rednecks had phoned in UFO sightings, I knew I had to find a fix for that, too.

The Grinder can destroy you and your family. Long hours and extreme stress lead to mistakes. And mistakes can lead to burn-out and defeat. Many people trying to work their way through The Grinder end up pushing away from the table, swearing they cannot eat another bite! But if you will hang in there, you'll find you can make it through to the end where your plate is empty but your heart is full. A word of caution here: take the time to look around you. You may be so focused on finishing this sandwich that you lose sight of the fact that your family might have already left the table! There must be a balance.

THE UPSIDE OF BEING LAZY

If my father could think of a way to do something faster, better, and easier, he was all over it. I inherited that same gene. I don't mind saying: I am fundamentally lazy. If I can create a shortcut to get the result I need, especially in repetitive tasks, I get busy making a workaround. This talent for leveraging my lethargy would serve me well throughout my career.

Part of the banality at Motorola involved making monthly call sheets that listed all the customers I'd contacted via long distance on my dime so I could get reimbursed for expenses. Back then, kiddos, we had to enter a credit card number whenever we wanted to make a long distance call. I spent hours on end matching up phone numbers on the company phone bill with my call sheets. I turned in a handwritten expense sheet at the end of every month. Sometimes it was just easier to eat some of the expenses because it took so darn long to wade through my poorly taken notes.

I decided one day to buy a computer with one of my bonus checks at Motorola. I went to my local RadioShack and bought the TRS-80, the first computer Tandy Corporation ever sold in stores. It was amazing because it used cassette tapes to store programs and data. But I needed it to be more flexible to suit my purposes. I tinkered with the inner workings of the BASIC language on our kitchen table until I was able to create a database of all the customers I talked to. When the next company phone bill came out, I simply typed in the phone numbers, and the computer spat out a line with the person's name, date, and amount owed me.

I could hardly sleep I was so excited. I proudly turned in my dot matrix printed call log sheet to Irene in Motorola's financial office in Dallas the next day. Irene stared at it expressionless for a minute as smoke curled from her lit cigarette. In her three-pack-a-day smoker's voice she grumbled, "I can't take this," as if I had handed her my second-grade spelling homework full of errors.

"Okayyyyy. Why not?" I asked and smiled patiently.

"It's not in your handwriting," she replied matter-of-factly and ceremoniously handed the sheet back to me.

"I know! Isn't that great?" I told her, sliding the document back to her across her desk. Then I really threw her off. "I wrote a computer program to make this list."

Irene squinted her eyes at this revelation, nonplussed.

"No you didn't," she insisted, wrinkling her nose.

"Oh, yes I did! Would it make you happy if I copied this print-out and put it in my handwriting?" I asked, maybe a little sarcastically.

Irene grumbled a sigh, and I left the sheet with her.

The next week, I got a check in the mail for my expenses. I have to say I enjoyed blowing Irene's mind that day. Computers were going to change everything, I reminded myself as I walked out of her office. Programs like Electric Pencil and Lotus 1-2-3 were going to alter the way the world worked. And it was barely even 1980.

It would just be a matter of time before technological advances would speed up to a rapid rate. In the meantime, I had to have patience, but I learned from this experience that designing and writing software to make my life easier was a really cool thing.

HAVING PATIENCE

You can add condiments to just about any type of food to make it more palatable. Salt, ketchup, or mayonnaise go a long way toward helping you get down something that's less than appetizing. Likewise, patience is a "condiment" that comes in handy when you're faced with a Failure Sandwich like The Grinder—it will help it go down smoother and give you some perspective when years of difficult work stretch out before you way longer than you anticipated.

That's the thing about time. It requires patience. In the moment that anything is happening in our lives, time goes by slowly. When you're 15, you can't wait to be 18. When you are in college, you can't wait to get out. When you marry, you can't wait to have kids. And on it goes. But when you look back on your life, you realize how quickly all of it—the good and the bad—goes by.

We can learn to take everything that happens to us in The Grinder years in stride when we see it in the light of eternity. A single event at work can be devastating— from a bad review, to a company restructuring, even bankruptcy. Even something personal like depression or an illness that lasts many years is horrible when we're going through it.

But think about it this way. If you live to see 80 or 90 years, that event will be in small proportion to your whole life. To a child that's five years old, one year is one-fifth of his or her whole life. That's a lot. At 68 years of age, however, one bad year is just one sixty-eighth of my total time on Earth. If this year does not turn out to be a good one, it's such a small percentage of your existence that you can get past it and look forward to things getting better.

Going without a job, for example, doesn't last forever, although it can feel that way—especially during something like a pandemic. A break-up, getting fired, or going through divorce can make it seem like life is over, but remember that the God who has no beginning and no end is the same one who can help you make a new start. Even the very worst events can be gut-wrenching but bearable when we realize this life isn't all there is.

If you just thought, "Phil's nuts," then read on. It may get crazier for you, but hang with me.

WHAT IS "TIME," REALLY?

In God's vocabulary, there is no such thing as "time." The concept of time was created for us as humans because we're hardwired to think only in terms of beginnings and endings. But walk with me down the "what if" road. What if there really is no beginning and no end? We quickly experience brain freeze when we try to conceive of something without a beginning or an end. It's hard for us to measure something without these benchmarks. So, God helped us out and described the opening act of Creation in Genesis and the end of time in Revelation for the benefit of finite individuals like us. Likewise, "Alpha and Omega" are terms that God uses to describe himself just to get the point across to us that he is the A-Z. He is infinite and exists outside of time altogether.

The Bible says in Ecclesiastes that God has set eternity in our hearts. As a dad myself, I can understand why he did that. I think it has to do with teaching us to keep life in perspective, which is crucial to making it through The Grinder years because the temptation is to wrap up so much of your identity in your job. At that stage, it's often all you think about.

I used to test my kids' brains (and their patience) whenever we made road trips, and it drove them nuts.

"All right," I'd tell them. "Who can think the farthest out in space? What's the farthest thing out there?"

After a minute, someone would shout, "Pluto!" This was back in the day when Pluto was a planet, the iPhone had not yet been invented, and families actually talked to each other in the car.

And then I'd say, "Okay, what's after that?"

"The Milky Way!" someone else would volunteer.

"All right. And after that?"

"Daaaad!" they would collectively moan.

I loved it.

I didn't love driving my kids crazy (okay, maybe a little), but I liked getting my kids to use their minds in a new way. I wanted them to stretch and think beyond themselves. This kind of out-of-the-box thinking is what drives all creativity. It's true—the brain is a muscle that must be exercised. Try it sometime. Let your mind think past what you can see right now. Don't be like Irene who couldn't imagine something new.

Forget the news headlines, the facts, and all that seems to be limiting you in some way. What are the possibilities that might happen in the future that might benefit you? When we learn to rely on God's limitless nature to guide our limited mind and life, many of our dreams we thought were absolutely impossible start coming true before our eyes—which was exactly what was about to happen to me.

FOUR

The Patty Melt

S ometimes you don't want to know what's under all that cheese. Not all patties in The Patty Melt are made of the same thing, if you know what I mean. I call this time in my life The Patty Melt because, like all jobs, there were elements of my work as a Motorola sales guy that I enjoyed more than others. You never know what you're going to get with The Patty Melt, and you find yourself either pleasantly surprised or disappointed.

I was happy at Motorola, but when I was in my late twenties, technology had evolved to a certain point and gave me a choice that would determine the rest of my career. Trunking was the way of the future, and one of my customers made me an offer in 1981 regarding this new technology that proved hard to turn down. I'd sold a 400-foot tower and a radio system to a customer in Kilgore who owned Rainbow Drilling. Robert wanted me to leave Motorola to help him create our own tower rental and trunking business. I balked at first. I had a solid career and a growing family.

My first child, Jenny, was born in 1978, and Mandy, my second child, was born in 1979. I loved being a dad. Jenny was born in a hospital in Longview, at a time when dads were not allowed in delivery rooms. (I have always been a guy who was pushing envelopes. I grew up in a day when girls were not allowed to wear slacks to our high school. When I served on our student council, I argued for girls to be allowed to wear skirts or slacks if they so chose.) When a couple of other guys in our birthing classes learned that we would NOT be allowed to be by our wives' sides, we worked with the hospital staff to change the rule. I was proud to be among the first husbands admitted into the delivery room and saw the miracle take place with my own eyes.

I just wish I had read a better textbook on how to do babies and kids. I look at my adult children now, who are amazing parents of their own kids, and I wonder how I ever made it. I had never been around babies before I had my own. I grew up as an only child, for all practical purposes. We parented in the days before the wonder of disposable diapers. It was all we could do to stay ahead of the next diaper change and budget for the next grocery run to keep feeding four mouths.

When you're single, you can eat Ritz crackers and live in a box. I happily lived on only ten bucks a week for food and ate a lot of pancakes. But now providing for my family was squarely on my mind, and the work at Motorola was safe and reliable. I had insurance, for goodness' sake, and the company Christmas party to look forward to. Why would I want to give up all that to go out on a limb for a business venture?

It didn't make sense. There was no way I was going to leave a good paying job and risk my job security and a career that was skyrocketing at Motorola. But sometimes, stepping out on faith is the most logical thing you can do, no matter how afraid you might feel inside.

SHOW ME THE CASHFLOW!

It took me two months before I gave Robert my answer. Five days into the new year, I resigned from Motorola and started a two-way radio tower and trunking business we called Jecca Towers about a month later. Once again, I left my previous job at Motorola on good terms.

One of my customers with Jecca Towers happened to be KLTV in Tyler, my former employer. I sold and installed their 1000-foot tower in Red Springs, Texas, using a contractor to build the tower structure but leaving the wiring as my own responsibility. I often found my happy place spending hours on top of the metal structure, catching glimpses of the tiny cars and cows on the earth below as I busily wired up the power and data for their tower, mostly by myself.

About two years into the business, Robert hired an in-house CPA named Ron. Ron called me into his office one day and told me to close the door and sit. That was a clue that things might not go well. Ron had a whiney voice and after ten seconds of small talk and never looking up from the desk he said, "Ehhhh we're going to close down Robert's business units that are not profitable."

I was shocked. "I know we're not profitable yet, Ron. But we are working our business plan," I replied.

"Well, you don't have any cashflow either," he whined, "and I don't see a future for Jecca."

I fumed in my head for about three seconds, jumped to my feet, started poking my finger through the top of his desk and blurted, "I BEG YOUR PARDON! WE HAVE CASHFLOW! IT'S NEGATIVE, BUT WE HAVE CASHFLOW!" and stormed out of his office.

Nine short and furiously busy years later, with the help of four employees, Robert and I built a highly successful rental tower and trunking company that grew from zero to 60% cash flow. Keeping 60 cents out of every dollar won't hurt you, but this level of success came at a price. Take that, CPA Ron! Entrepreneurship is definitely its own kind of The Patty Melt because it has good things and bad things associated with it, and you never know which ones you're going to experience on a certain day. Like every entrepreneur experiencing growing pains, I was also chief baker and candlestick maker, in addition to being a co-founder of Jecca Towers. I worked incredibly long hours to get to this point. Once again, I did not spend the time I wanted at home with my young family. My wife and I separated and ultimately divorced in early 1985.

WORKING HARD AT BEING LAZY

We were making money off the trunking systems, but we were also building those thin skyscrapers for ourselves and other companies at the same time, while also creating invoices and maintaining our profit margins. We had a tower construction crew, but toward the end of this venture, it was just me and one assistant.

I work hard at being lazy, you'll recall. So one day while creating yet another set of invoices, I thought, "There's got to be a better way to do this." I found my inspiration in the IBM Displaywriter system, the earliest word processing computer that was designed for office use. This machine was a beauty and featured a lovely giant green tube display. Its hefty keyboard issued a loud clatter with every keystroke.

On nights and weekends, I'd work in the office and tweak the code of the Displaywriter, hoping to create a more convenient billing process for my own purposes. I had taught myself everything I knew about programming. Sure, the software I came up with had its share of quirks and workarounds, but I was fine with that for my use. It did what I needed it to do. However, to my surprise, some people who were also in the trunking business began expressing interest in buying the software program. So I set about stepping up my game. I rewrote it to a professional level and named it EZBill because that's exactly what it was—an easier way to bill customers.

I sold my first EZBill software program to a man who owned a tower and trunking company in the small Texas town of Big Springs for the grand sum of $995. I was nervous. The experience was like selling a car that you've performed all the maintenance on yourself. You know that car. It's your baby. You know what it needs. You know what its sensitivities are. I discovered it was the same way with my software. I had to translate familiar idiosyncrasies into a professional instruction manual detailing exactly how to run the program step-by-step. I had never written a tech manual before, much less for something I created myself! I really wished I had paid more attention in English class!

I drove out to Big Springs, installed the software, and trained the customer as thoroughly as possible on how to use it. I then made the drive home with a check in hand, along with the deep satisfaction of having a happy customer who appreciated the convenience as much as I did! The next EZBill customer owned a trunking system in Terminal—another West Texas town aptly named after the airport terminal near Midland—and he immediately saw how EZBill could make his life easier, too.

Word continued to spread. When you make something that customers need, understand, and like, you become a popular guy. As it happens, there were other inherently lazy people like me always wanting to save time doing mundane tasks. I began wondering if this invention of mine just might have a future.

A LINE IN THE SAND

When I met and married Bobbie, I discovered that life wasn't over after my divorce. I had a wonderful wife and partner by my side and three beautiful children, including Bobbie's daughter, Ally, from an earlier marriage. We believed the best could still be yet to come. I had (and can at times still have) the habit of allowing myself to drag baggage of the past along with me. But I remembered one of the best pieces of advice my father gave me. He was clear to say it was not original to him, but it helped him with similar "baggage dragging" moments. The advice? "Draw a line, and go from there." Couldn't be more simple and more profound.

When we married, Bobbie and I drew a line in the sand—literally. The past was the past. We wanted to claim God's forgiveness for previous mistakes and take him up on his offer of a second chance. This is a leap of faith to believe that's even possible, and it's difficult for humans to make that leap for some reason.

But the offer is available to everyone and so simple for him to do. To be clear, God's love and forgiveness is no guarantee of a bump-free road. No sir! What it does give you is a place to go when that road seems unbearable, like when the hot cheese from your Patty Melt cascades onto your hands and life becomes a royal mess.

About the time EZBill was picking up speed, a couple of buddies of mine had a proposition. I had met Morgan at one of the trade shows, and we struck up a professional relationship over the years as we ended up on the same non-profit boards in our industry. He was an attorney with a techie side that led him to also delve into the trunking world. He and his business partner began purchasing trunking systems across the United States. They had cash and made lucrative offers to the early pioneering mom-and-pop entrepreneurs. These two men would eventually form Nextel, the first company to offer a nationwide push-to-talk system.

Nextel expressed an interest in buying Jecca Towers as one of their acquisitions. Robert and I talked about it and agreed to let them make us an offer. They did so, and it was an okay offer, but it wasn't great. This wasn't the end of the story for my relationship with Nextel. We would cross paths again down the road.

Robert and I then shopped around and gathered a few more offers from interested parties, including Motorola, after some former associates heard Jecca Towers might be looking to sell. When Robert told me one day that Motorola had contacted him and made an offer that was twice the amount Nextel offered, I thought about it for exactly one minute.

"Ummmm, yes!" I said, sitting in a chair in his office. "Let's accept it."

There was a time when I had wanted to buy out my partner and become principal owner of Jecca Towers, but I did not know how I would pull that off financially. Thank goodness that risky option didn't work out. When Motorola bought our company, instead of having a huge debt strung around my neck, I would have money in the bank.

When we met with Motorola to review their purchase, we went over a complex list of assets, including towers, generators, and so on. At the bottom of the document I listed "software," meaning EZBill, since it had technically been written on Jecca's time and thus it was a Jecca asset.

"What's this software?" the representative from Motorola wanted to know. "What should be done with that?" It was a poignant question and one that, depending on the way I answered it, held far-reaching consequences.

I've done three really smart things in my life so far. The first is following Christ by faith. The second is asking Bobbie to marry me. The third has to be my answer to the Motorola rep's question that day.

"It depends on if you want to have the liability for it," I said without batting an eye. There, I'd said it, the dreaded "four-letter word" in negotiations: liability. It hung in the air as we all looked around the table at each other.

The rep didn't want to touch that, so he left EZBill off

the table, and with Robert's blessing I retained the rights to EZBill for myself. After all, I knew the liability—I wrote the thing.

A NEW BEGINNING CALLED GENESIS

By 1989 I had been married to Bobbie a few years, we had money in our account, and I was the happiest technically unemployed man around. It was a scary, wonderful time. Bobbie left a longstanding career in radio broadcasting to start a great marketing and advertising company. I was toying around with the idea of turning EZBill into the frontrunner software offering of my own new company. We talked about our ideas for the future in the car, after dinner, before breakfast, virtually anytime we were together—as great partners and teammates tend to do. We tossed around timelines and chewed on potential company names. One day we stopped in the middle of one these brainstorming sessions in our living room and prayed. All we did was ask our Best Friend for guidance. He could see the future; we could not. Minutes after that, we resumed our conversation, and it was apparent there was a new sense of direction and purpose behind our words.

A little context. This season in our lives was a fresh beginning for both of us in many ways. We had a new family of five, a new marriage, and two new companies in the works. When the word, "genesis," came out of our mouths at about the same time, The Genesis Group was born.

Bobbie supported my dream for EZBill, and the two
of us started driving to trade shows to drum up customers
in Florida and various locations. We were living on the
money from the Jecca Towers sale, which wasn't that
much in today's dollars. Little by little, we began building
up a customer base.

The birth of a company is not unlike the birth of a
child. There are times when you feel so darn proud of
what you created, and then there are times when you
want to tear your hair out in frustration. Again, it's The
Patty Melt—a Failure Sandwich that's full of surprises.
Success as a parent and a business owner comes with
both ecstasy and exhaustion. I remember once having
$5000 in bills sitting on my desk and exactly $157.00
in the company checkbook. It's that kind of moment that
can drive you to your knees. You can worry about a crisis,
or you can do something about it. I chose to pray, on my
knees.

I talked to God about the problem and told him I
thought the company was about to go under, unless he
stepped in and helped me. If this was the end of the
road for The Genesis Group, I told him, I was going to
be devastated, quite honestly. But I would ultimately be
okay with this decision, I added, and I meant that.

About ten minutes later, the phone rang from an
old Motorola friend, offering me a consulting job on a
new building being built in Nashville. How much was
it going to pay? Take a guess. Yep, exactly $5000. I

swallowed hard and asked him if there was any way for me to receive half of the money upfront, which he gladly overnighted to me the next day. That consulting job was related to what is now fondly called the Batman Building in Nashville. Business didn't take off immediately after that; nor did this event magically solve all my problems. But the unexpected cash staved off closing our doors prematurely.

If you're a business owner, you don't have to wait for a crisis. It will find you soon enough. If you're a parent, student, or just someone trying to make it through life, you are probably going through a big problem or just coming out of one. Life takes prayer. Patty Melts go down easier with prayer. Similar to having patience, prayer is another "condiment" to put on any Failure Sandwich to help you sit down and get through a crisis one bite at a time. Like salt, prayer adds a powerful and unique dimension to any situation.

Prayer can change outcomes. And it provides power and peace. The answer doesn't always happen with dramatic, immediate effect like the story I shared about the Batman Building consulting job. But it happens often enough for me to know that it's a wise move to operate my life and my company for the approval of Someone I rely on daily for direction and guidance. This is just one of hundreds of stories I could tell where my Best Friend took care of me, my family, and our company.

A GROWING LINE OF SOFTWARE

For a long time, I was the sole member of the software side of The Genesis Group. The first hire I made was out of necessity because I needed someone to write code in a language I did not speak. Greg was my inaugural employee—a young, single guy banging out code at his kitchen counter in his apartment. Contract workers are a great way to try out someone to see if they're a good fit because you do not have the associated tax liability of an employee. I liked his work, and he liked what we were doing. Over the next 20 years, we added many new employees, and Greg was still with us.

EZBill was selling very well at this point, so The Genesis Group next created EZSave, a simplified way of communicating with various trunking systems. These software programs sold themselves because they made sense, and they worked. We named our line of software "EZ" for a reason. I wanted to create an easier way for our customers to do business. In this case, that meant not having to remember a long string of commands to communicate between trunking systems. EZSave software let the computers do the heavy lifting.

Nextel was running about 1,800 trunking systems at the time and also needed an efficient way to manage all their systems. Ironically, many of the trunking systems they had acquired nationwide were also already running EZBill, and my buddies at Nextel took note of this. They eventually approached me about purchasing EZBill and EZSave to help manage their systems, and I made one of the biggest sales for The Genesis Group to date in 1992. This was big stuff, and I wanted to celebrate with everyone who had taken part in this journey so far. We were still in survival mode, but we took the handful of employees we had at The Genesis Group out to a barbeque joint between Tyler and Kilgore called The Country Tavern. Teamwork was a core value that I made sure I continued to celebrate in the future.

Whenever I provided support for my customers, it was almost always conducted over the phone. Forget Facetime, Google Hangout, or screen sharing. This was in the prehistoric times before all that. I knew from my early experience selling EZBill that phone support had its perils. This was back in the DOS days, mind you, so software programming was tedious and complicated. Customers would tell me on the phone that they were on the main menu, but I knew from what they were describing to me that they weren't REALLY on the main menu. They just thought they were.

To ensure we were all on the same page when I provided phone support, I built unique sounds into our programs. Whenever customers landed on certain pages within the menu, the computer running the software would make a distinctly audible cue that I could hear and pinpoint exactly where they were. When I flew to Northern New Jersey to install the software for both EZ programs at the Nextel headquarters, I spent considerable time with the billing department and never tired of hearing the beautiful sound of an orchestra of cubicles emitting these "dings" and "kerplunks."

I smiled the grin of a proud parent. "This stuff really works," I said to myself as I got on the elevator and went to my hotel for the night after a long day of troubleshooting and training. But it was just the start of even more cool stuff for The Genesis Group.

EZBILL GAINS NEW CUSTOMERS

Genesis had been in business a little over three years when I was contacted by a Motorola guy named Dan working in Melbourne, Australia. It was around 1993, and I remember wondering how he first heard about our little company, especially from the other side of the world. They had issues with their current billing system because it was designed for traditional telephone billing and had its limitations. When he named the wish-list features they needed and wanted a billing system to do, I knew EZBill came close to meeting his needs, or at least closer than what they had in place.

Over the course of a few months, using painfully slow dial-up modems, I made modifications to EZBill and loaded the software to their server in Australia. Then after many late-night conversations (late according to my time zone), it was time for me to fly to Oz to finally meet Dan's Motorola team and put this EZBill program to work.

This event Down Under marked the beginning of Genesis' official relationship with Motorola. Dan believed in Genesis. He and I built a close working and personal relationship in those early years, even after he relocated to Hawaii (his current home). As I acquired clients in Hawaii, I often visited him and his wife when I was in the Islands. It was always a sweet reunion! Dan is one of the big reasons that today we work so closely with Motorola all around the globe.

I eventually sold and installed EZBill and EZSave for Motorola's International Network Services, and we picked up 30-40 clients in other countries. I was soon boarding more international flights than I'd ever imagined, traveling throughout the world to install the software and provide training, while racking up 1.2 million frequent flyer miles.

I often had to rewrite the code to suit the particular needs of the clients in whatever country I happened to be in that week. I remember being in the Bahamas one week training 10 wonderful Bahamian ladies on the EZBill system for the Bahamas Telephone Company. For the first two days of the week, we did very basic training on how to do the billing for their two Motorola trunking systems. The ladies took notes and listened very intently to what I had to say. By mid-week, I announced to the women that it was hands-on day. I picked one of them to sit behind the keyboard as the others gathered around to watch. This was back in the DOS days, so I had her push "F" for "Files." And we discussed the information on the screen.

"Okay, now go back to the main menu," I told her.

Silence. The sentence at the bottom of the screen said, "Press any key to return to the main menu."

"Go ahead. Do what the screen says," I encouraged her.

"I'm trying to do what the screen says," she said in her thick, Bahamian accent. "But I cannot find the Any key anywhere."

It happened to me. And it was Wednesday. I was leaving in two days! In half an hour that night back at the hotel, I searched through the code and replaced "any key" with "Enter/Return." I recompiled it and we continued our training the next day. Problem solved.

Another time, their Freeport office called me in September to tell me they had "a little invoice problem."

"What kind of problem?" I wanted to know.

"We haven't been able to invoice since May," they said. I wondered why they hadn't called me sooner, but in traditional island style, they did not seem too worried about it! They asked if I would come to Freeport to work on the issue. I made sure to include my wife on these frequent trips so that while I was working she could enjoy some time off. It was a beautiful place.

The day I arrived, I went to their office and started working in the closet-sized room where their billing computer and printer was. I started going through the usual checkpoints, looking at their hard disk space, etc. Nothing was wrong. I was stumped. I looked at the printer, felt around on the side for the power switch and, yep...turned it on.

Immediately, the printer started spitting out invoices. Five months of invoices, to be exact. Seriously, you can't make this stuff up.

I was once in Sao Paulo, Brazil, making my way through a marathon code-writing day that was broken up by the delivery of cute, tiny cups of coffee from the office staff throughout the afternoon.

"How nice of them!" I thought and sipped six of the little things in a few hours before I knew any better.

At three in the morning, I was still happily pounding out code left and right at my hotel. Frankly, I was amazed by my level of productivity. I was Superman, flying through my workload. When I returned home to Texas the next day, I hit the treadmill and suddenly felt as if I were having a heart attack! I was jittery and clammy. Alarmed, I went to see my doctor and there learned about the perils of Brazilian espresso and the reality of caffeine withdrawal. I missed my superpowers, but not the shakes!

Like all growing businesses, there were stops, starts, and moments that tried my patience with this new venture with Motorola. I'll never forget working with Dave and Dave, two Motorola guys that were with a joint client of ours in Ecuador. "Dave S" called me one day to say, "Phil, we have a problem. Someone has hacked into your EZBill program." This was a Failure Sandwich I never expected having to sit down and eat. It was a Patty Melt for sure because it made me sick to my stomach immediately.

THE TWO DAVES

I was alarmed, but I tried to stay calm. "Tell me what you're seeing," I said, balancing the phone between my ear and shoulder as I turned to my computer screen at my desk in Texas.

"Dave S" then explained that in the process of coming back to the main menu, a nefarious blank screen had popped up with a cryptic text in the middle.

"What does it say?" I asked, hesitant to hear the answer. My mind raced through the possibilities. Was it pornographic? Was it a terrorist threat? What was it?

"Well, it's weird," he responded. "It says, 'God Loves You.'"

I relaxed when I heard this. I had built that message into the software to buy a few milliseconds of time. In programming parlance, I had to buy those milliseconds to clean up the memory-heap in the program. I'd purposely typed what I considered to be an innocuous message in the coding: God Loves You. No client had ever seen it before, or if they had seen it, they had not notified me.

"I put that in there," I told him, chuckling.

He paused before answering, "Well, I don't know if we can leave that in there."

It was my turn to pause now. "What do you mean? Is that an order for me to take it out?"

He went on to say that I needed to remove this message from the software if we were going to continue to do international business together. I saw his point and reluctantly agreed to comply. I recompiled the program, figured out a different way to kill a few milliseconds in a different way, and sent the update to him.

And then a strange thing happened. My business dried up over the next three months. The phone did not ring. I had zero sales.

It was a little thing I'd done that carried a big consequence. I have always felt it was more important to honor God with the little things, since I had my eye on bigger things down the road. I had promised God he could trust me with the little things, so that he could trust me with the big things. Yep, I had failed on my own promise. I made up my mind and picked up the phone.

I called Dave S and his colleague "Dave Y" while they were in their offices at Motorola's headquarters. I told them I was going to re-install the God Loves You message, and if that action lost their business, so be it.

We were on speakerphone, and they both sat silent for a long time. "Well, Phil," Dave Y said to me, "why don't you just put it where it belongs then?"

"Where is that?" I wanted to know, expecting some

snarky reply.

"On the main menu," came the unexpected response. "Put it there."

They explained that it wasn't the words but the subliminal nature of the message that threw up a red flag for the company execs. But if I agreed to put the message on the main menu, they said it could stay.

I did not understand what I was hearing, but I was all in. I felt a wave of relief, embarrassment, and wanting to cry all at once. I recompiled the program for a second time and sent it to the client, my message of love firmly planted on the main menu.

At the risk of not being believed, I have to say that sales started coming in again for The Genesis Group after that. Was it a coincidence? You can say so. I'm putting my money on the fact that something else was at work. My point to this story is this: convictions are what you believe in—or they're nothing at all. Whatever decisions you make in life, stand by them. Be willing to fight for them.

I ended up spending many hours on the phone after that with the two Daves as we planned and built out how our software would operate in countries like the Czech Republic, Venezuela, Brazil, Ecuador, India, and many more. I ended up traveling to about 10 countries to install and train the EZBill suite of software.

On one trip to Caracas, I finished the day and went to the restaurant in the Intercontinental Hotel for dinner. I had just started my meal when I saw a tall American guy walk down the steps into the restaurant. I could see he wore a Motorola badge, and when he got closer, I read his name and called out, "Dave!"

Dave Y and I had never physically met, nor did we have any idea we were both in Caracas, let alone staying in the same hotel and going to eat at the same place, at the same time! He joined me at my table, and we eventually got around to the topic of how traveling the world can take a toll on families. Dave related how it had cost him his first marriage. Feeling comfortable in our conversation, he even shared how depressed he was after his divorce. And he told me an astonishing story.

"I was depressed for much more than a few hours here or there after my divorce," he told me. "Relatives and some friends said I needed to get back into a church where I could find new friends. I finally broke down one Sunday and went to a small church that I had passed many times. As I pulled into the property, it was a few minutes after 11:00am. The sign said the service started at 11:00, and the parking lot was full. I was late and made up my mind to simply pull out and go back home."

Matter-of-factly he continued, "There was a guy in a blue jumpsuit sort of outfit who was watering the flowers. He motioned to me. 'Just park here on the grass, nobody will mind,' he said. I explained that I knew I was late and likely wouldn't find a seat, but he implored me to go on in and he would go with me. I went in, found a seat, but never did see the guy in the blue jumpsuit again. The sermon that day and a reception after church was a turning point in my life!"

I sat, listening intently while my eyes grew huge. Dave asked what I was thinking. I said "Dave, what church would have a gardener watering flowers during a church service on a Sunday morning? I'm pretty sure you had an encounter with an angel!"

It took Dave about four seconds, his eyes darting back and forth, to consider this possibility. As he recounted the story and other events, it was like a club hit him. He threw himself against the back of his chair and almost yelled, "Oh my word! That's it! It had to be an angel! There's no other explanation." There is even much more to this story that I'm not including that proves this encounter was no coincidence.

Look around you. There is more to The Patty Melt than meets the eye. Things that come across as coincidence maybe deserve a second look. Is God working on your behalf, and you're just not seeing it?

TO THE RESCUE!

With the success of our first two software programs, we continued adding software that made business easier for our customers. We next created EZTrac, a software that graphically showed performance data for every trunking system. The Genesis Group was graphing on DOS computer systems when that kind of thing just wasn't done.

Then came along a new thing called Windows. With each new software we created, and each new technological advance, The Genesis Group needed to add more people to our team. A programmer named Michael was part of The Genesis Group by then, and I tasked him with making some of our old DOS-based software graphically appealing to the new "Windows hippies," as I called them. He wrote EZTrac for Windows, and we renamed it GenWatch, which became another very successful offering in our growing line of software.

We built an entire business out of selling creative solutions that no one else could or would provide. I remember wanting to run an ad for The Genesis Group that compared us to a giant caulking gun. We were constantly filling in the gaps for customers who could not get what they wanted any other way. I told people to think of us like the JC Whitney catalog of aftermarket accessories to pimp your ride for truck owners. There's the basic truck you buy at a dealership from the big automaker, and then you get all the super cool things you want from the smaller guy, JC Whitney. We saw ourselves like that. Customers wanted niche software that other bigger tech companies could not justify putting into their catalog of wares.

Motorola continued to be an important client for The Genesis Group in those early years. They consistently turned to us for software solutions and highly recommended us to others in the industry. I sometimes attended Motorola meetings to keep in close communication with them and to be attentive to their trends and needs. Most of the time I listened far more than I spoke at those meetings. We didn't need the spotlight on Genesis—we wanted to make the Motorolans of the world look like heroes to their customers. Of course, the more problems we solved for clients, the more we looked like heroes to Motorola. This is how it works. You help people get what they need, and the customers will come to you.

When a high-dollar contract between Motorola and a concrete company stalemated, The Genesis Group got to work coming up with a solution that satisfied both parties. The Motorola customer was facing a necessary system upgrade with a serious downside. No customer likes change, especially when it threatens someone's sense of business as usual. In this case, the status message system that allowed concrete truck drivers to push a single button on the radio to notify the main office whenever they picked up and poured a load was tied into their automated billing system. That would all stop working with Motorola's upgrade, and Motorola wasn't sure they could put it back the way it was because the original set up was all hardcoded by a long-departed Motorola employee.

Worse yet, no one could find the source code to figure out how he'd done it. It was the Mack Truck Syndrome. If the one person who knows how something works is hit by a Mack truck one day, all that information dies with that person! It's not a good way to run a business, but it happens all the time because information is evolving, and the work is transacted at the speed of light these days.

At Motorola's request, Michael and I poked around and sniffed the data packets to figure out what was going on in the existing system. He wrote a solution, while I guided the process. We had no idea if it would work, but we reinstalled it, and to our delight it did the job. Motorola became a hero for the concrete company. And we ingratiated ourselves to Motorola, who in return fully licensed us in the process to use some of their technology we'd been "borrowing" up to that point—all because we got them out of a jam.

THE (PATTY) MELTDOWN

The future seemed bright for our partnership with Motorola until a day came when the granddaddy of all Patty Melts landed on my plate. It was served to me in a very unappetizing way, and I did NOT enjoy the surprise under all the bubbling cheese!

I was summoned from Texas to a meeting at the Motorola headquarters located at that time in a Chicago suburb. We were living in the post-9/11 world, and public safety was on everyone's minds. One of the biggest failures of 9/11 was that the fire department couldn't talk with the police department, who couldn't talk with the ambulances, who couldn't talk with power companies, and the list went on. Project 25 (or P25 as it was nicknamed) was a digital mobile radio communications solution designed for public safety organizations and first responders to better communicate. Radios and handheld walkie-talkies were the central features of P25, and the program drastically changed the telecommunications business in a positive way.

The Genesis Group made a host of compatible software enhancements for P25, and I was looking forward to continuing the lucrative partnership with Motorola. That was before I found myself walking into an unforeseen and unwelcome set of circumstances at the 9:00am meeting with several Motorola executives in their Schaumburg, Illinois, headquarters.

I sat in the boardroom only 15 minutes before I was back in my hotel room, staring blankly at the wall and wondering, "What in the WORLD just happened in there?"

I was in no way prepared for the bad news I'd heard come out of their mouths. It hit me like a sucker punch.

"Phil," they'd said, "this meeting is just to let you know Motorola is not going to use you for any of the future P25 products."

Those words sank in. Work we had already done for P25 was dead. The next 15 years of business was gone.

The executives then explained that they were

planning to do all their product development in-house, which made sense for them but was a crushing blow to The Genesis Group. That's why they called me all the way up to Chicago—to tell me in person that they no longer needed me.

I picked up the phone in my room and called my team back in Tyler to break the news. "It doesn't look good," I told them in no uncertain terms.

I left the hotel, got on a plane, and started the long journey back home to Tyler. On the way, a long-forgotten memory from grade school popped in my mind and taught me a lesson I'll explain in the next chapter.

FIVE

The Colossal

She's long dead, so I'll call her by her real name: Miss Yoder. She was a teacher—thin, dark hair, tall, and she was old although she was only probably in her twenties. I was in second grade at the time, so everyone was tall and old to me. The connection we shared was music class. Miss Yoder would take our hands and place them on the piano keys to help us play a series of random notes. Then she'd say, "Sing me one note out of that."

It was a pretty good idea. If a kid can find one note out of a series of gobbledygook musically speaking, and sing it on pitch, he or she likely has a propensity for music. I couldn't read quickly and I struggled in multiplication, but I could always find the note Miss Yoder wanted. I felt an enormous sense of pride, but Miss Yoder didn't seem to return the feeling.

I remember being on the playground one day and overhearing Miss Yoder talking about me. "Phil is stupid. He'll never amount to anything, that kid," I heard her remark to the fellow teachers in earshot of other students as they walked arm-in-arm together around the perimeter of the playground. I was devastated. To make matters worse, some of my closest friends also overheard what she said.

I know now that I probably had ADD (Attention Deficit Disorder) as a child and am definitely dyslexic—but back then they did not have those terms for children. Many of us were incorrectly and not-so-scientifically labeled as just having "ants in your pants."

"That was really stupid, Phil," Miss Yoder told me on more than one occasion after that day whenever I made a mistake on my homework or came up with the wrong answer to a question. And sometimes it wasn't actually said aloud. It was just that look and the slight movement of her head from side to side, telegraphing her thoughts on my stupidity.

In addition to being dyslexic, I'm left-handed, so everything was goofy for me while learning to write and do math problems. From the fifth grade onward, I practically begged my teachers to let me take tests orally, instead of having to write down my answers. It never happened, so I learned to struggle through and figure out how to do my work. Dyslexia is something that pops in and out of numbers and words all day and wreaks havoc on daily activities. But, like everything else, you deal. To this day I'm a slow reader. I like to say I'm savoring the words to nuance the content. But I'm slow. And I'm learning to be okay with that.

If people were honest, I think you'd find that many grown adults still trip over negative stuff that happened to them, or was said about them, when they were kids. This chapter is about a special kind of Failure Sandwich: The Colossal. I call this Failure Sandwich The Colossal because rejection is huge. It takes most people a long time to process pain adequately and get to a point in life where they're at peace with their past.

This variety of Failure Sandwich is unique because it doesn't have anything to do with an actual mistake YOU made or a failure on YOUR part! It's something hurtful someone ELSE said about you that makes you feel like a failure. The Colossal is about rejection in one form or another. It's believing something negative that you understand to be true about yourself. It's the terrible experience you had in your past that haunts you. And it keeps you from reaching your full potential.

THE NUTCRACKER – NOT SO SUITE

Let me illustrate. On the way home to Tyler after the disastrous Motorola meeting, I had one of those "maybe Miss Yoder was right about me" flashbacks. Maybe I really *was* stupid, I told myself repeatedly.

This childhood memory wasn't the first time someone else had made me question my own ability and even doubt the very core of who I was. I recall being cast in the Nutcracker in early elementary school. I got the part of the Prince of the Dolls. At the pivotal moment in the classic play, my character would turn from a nutcracker into a prince.

The rest of the parts were divvied out that afternoon, and we were all charged with designing our own costumes. My family did not have a lot of money, so I had to get creative. For the first half of the play when I was a nutcracker, I decided to hold up a simple poster of a doll. The audience got the idea. For the prince, I had an idea in my head of the quintessential prince outfit: green leotards, jacket, and, of course, a gold crown.

"Leave it to me," I told my teacher when she asked what I planned to wear.

I went shopping with my mom and was shocked to discover green leotards were not nearly as ubiquitous in Levittown, Pennsylvania, as I'd assumed. There weren't any puff-sleeved jackets or crowns lying around the house either. Panic began to sink in.

A few days before the play, I rummaged through my chest of drawers and came up with the next closest thing: green corduroy pants. And someone in the neighborhood graciously loaned me a "crown" at the last minute. When I came out on stage dressed as the prince, everyone laughed and cat-called, but I wasn't sure why. Turns out, I hadn't borrowed a crown, per se, but something more like a tiara. I'm a guy. What did I know? This experience flattened me. Miss Yoder was right again. I wanted to crawl in a hole, my coping mechanism of choice even now as an adult.

Why do these childhood memories stick with me? I'm a man in my late sixties, shouldn't I be over this by now? The casual comment, "That was really stupid, Phil," uttered by a long-dead grade school teacher (and others who followed suit on occasion throughout my adult life) still haunts me. Why is that? The answer has to do with the fact that words have power. And it is extremely powerful to convey to someone—anyone—that they are somehow less than acceptable.

My parents never talked negatively about me while growing up, and both were extremely supportive throughout my life. If anything, they simply pushed me to do better when I made mistakes. Mom and Dad knew how much I struggled, but they told me over and over, "You can do anything," and "It's going to be ok." Stuff like that would bring me out of my hole every time I got down on myself.

"There's a plan for your life, and we just have to find out what that is," they'd remind me. One time they even offered to pay for pilot lessons when I was 12 years old to see if I wanted to follow in the footsteps of my missionary pilot hero, Bernie. I decided not to do it, knowing the cost might be more than my parents could comfortably afford. But it meant a lot to me that they thought I actually could do it and that they were even willing to fund that dream despite my dad's meager salary.

What I'm saying is that even with double-layer positivity from my parents, I still struggle with self-doubt because of what was said about me early on by others. After all this time, I struggle with imposter syndrome. At my core self is the stubborn belief that I'm not that smart. I'm married to a licensed professional counselor, so I know that self-doubt is part of what it means to be human. I also realize how likely it is that something similar has happened to you, too. You just need to be prepared to deal with it when it pops up so that negativity and self-doubt don't derail your potential and sabotage your life purpose.

THE POWER OF WORDS

You have to make your way through The Colossal one bite, one step at a time. You must be deliberate in how you personally deal with rejection—and take care to help others who might be at the table next to yours working on their own version of The Colossal.

One action you can take to turn this around is to surround yourself with positive people who will speak helpful, affirming words. And you can make it your aim to do the same for others. Commit right now to find something positive to say about everyone. For some people, it may require digging deep and looking extra hard, but you can find something affirming to say about everyone you encounter.

Be extremely cautious about what you say, especially with young, impressionable people who may work for you or alongside you. When you talk with people, be full of love. Most people are doing the best they can these days. All of us can learn to resist the temptation of sarcasm and passive aggressiveness. It goes against human nature, but we can fight against the pull to be nasty to someone who is nasty to us. I quickly raise my hand to admit that I'm speaking to myself on all these points.

When was the last time you thanked someone who took the time to speak affirming words to you? One of the most influential things you can do is to thank another person. Saying "thank you" when it's not natural for you to do so is a good exercise. You might even say something like, "You have no idea how what you said positively influenced my life..." And then tell your story. That's all it takes. It's a potent and simple thing for you to say, as well as for someone else to hear! And some people need to hear it weekly, daily, and even multiple times a day.

When you get down to it, all people want to know they're doing something right. Daniel Pink, in his book DRIVE, talks about how at our core, we deeply desire significance. We'll explore this part of The Colossal later on, but let me say now that I, for one, am built that way. There was a time in my life when I needed more validation in business than I do now. One of the reasons why I need less confirmation today is because I've lived long enough to see the fruit of my labor in other people's lives. I KNOW I've made progress toward achieving my purpose in life. The people who have left Genesis and turned into leaders and innovators at other companies are proof that we did our part right. It's like raising children. It's an honor when they turn out to be better people than you are! That's the highest compliment for a mom and dad. When your employees really want your job, don't be threatened by that. Take it as a compliment. When your team members go on to be bigger and better than you are, that's a good thing, and you ought to tell them so.

Words have tremendous power to influence people and situations. I've collected a list of what I call "Power Words" over the years. Many of these are used predominantly in social media and headlines to get our attention. Click bait is also a term for these magnetic words and phrases that, when used strategically, can turn the tide—many times in a bad direction.

I've learned to use the following Power Words *very* sparingly in writing and speaking because I don't want to manipulate others:

Startling
Shocking
BREAKING NEWS...
PANIC

Bombshell

Helpless

Brutal

Demolishes

Horrifying

Treasonous

Insane

Stunned

Disrupts

Reveals

EPIC

Then this happened...

Look what just happened...

Then he said this....

Then we noticed this...

The game just changed...

The TRUTH about...

Unbelievable

This will ruin him/her...

Now it's serious...

What he discovered is TERRIFYING...

This changes everything...

No one expected to see this...

It just gets worse.....

It turns out...

This is going to go viral....

___never saw THIS coming...

___ makes a HUGE move...

FREAKING out....

___ *sparked outrage...*

Scolding

As God transitioned me into a mentor role at work and in my community, I started reflecting on a few men in my life who invested positive words, wisdom, and kindness in me. For example, I've had the joy of thanking people like Neil Fichthorn, who mentored me when I was a young man in church, as well as crediting Nels Stjernstrom, who mentored me in college. For the past 30 years I have also been able to hang around with the amazing Mike Parks as he led our church choir and the entire worship ministry staff. He breathed words of encouragement into me when I needed that kick in the pants. And I've had the privilege of being there for him in his dark hours. You NEED people around you who will lovingly give you what you need to keep going.

Neil was my youth director, choir director, and mentor when I was growing up in Levittown. I wanted Neil to know how his influence on me as a teen helped shape me into the adult I am today. So, I wrote Neil to remind him of an incident that took place at Sandy Cove Bible Conference. I volunteered there several summers in high school as a defacto leader of the summer staff under Neil (most of whom were also young adults like me). Many of my peers felt that Neil was inconsistent in the way he handled his responsibilities. I remember one hot summer evening the staff members were all sitting around griping about Neil in typical teenager fashion just as he walked up to our group!

I was suddenly nominated as the spokesperson to tell him how everyone felt, so I did. Others chimed in, and things got heated. I'll never forget Neil's calculated response as he looked each of us in the eye and said, "I beg your pardon for disappointing you." And then his mouth twitched into a smile and he added, "I AM consistent! I am just consistently inconsistent!"

We all broke into laughter and instantly became much better friends and colleagues. I told myself then that I wanted to be more like Neil in leadership. A little well-placed humor can defuse a volatile situation, if done with taste.

When I played King Arthur as a senior at Woodrow Wilson High School, I invited Neil and his wife to see me perform one Friday night. I never saw him in the audience, but when I went to church youth group on Sunday, Neil did something unexpected. He told the entire class what a great job I'd done Friday. Then he invited me up to the front of the room to recite some impromptu lines from *Camelot*. Everyone applauded afterward, and it was one of those feel-good moments you don't easily forget. If you're old enough to know who Sally Field is, then you remember her 1985 Oscar acceptance speech where she enthusiastically told the audience, "I can't deny the fact that you like me! Right now, you like me!" It was like that with Neil and the class that day.

Needing validation as a leader is not wrong if people's feedback helps you see where you're doing okay leading the way forward and where you're doing the right stuff. If your motive as a leader is to have another person's admiration because you're a narcissist, that's different and flat wrong. It can be a slippery slope because you may find yourself surrounded only by "yes-men" just to puff up your ego. Be balanced in the voices you have around you. You need people who will gently show you weak and blind spots. In my case, I have a great range of voices, including those that help drown out the "you're not good enough" voice. Add a LOT of prayer and discussion with my Best Friend, and it seems to balance out.

It's never too late to give that gift of admiration and gratitude to express how you feel about someone who influences you and makes your life a little better. After my other mentor Nels Stjernstrom died, I wrote a letter to his son Jim. I told him several stories about all the ways his dad had made me feel important as a college student. Nels was a professor, advisor, author, and magazine editor at LeTourneau University. He modeled for me how to mentor someone, and I am forever grateful. Nels had a fizzy personality that could brighten any bad day! He had a way of looking me square in the eye and listening with every ounce of his being to what concerned me at that moment. Being a card-carrying, lifelong self-doubter, I told Jim how spending regular time with his dad carried me through my college years when I was thousands of miles away from my family.

For every cheerleader who learns to use words properly to edify others, you can count on naysayers and manipulators who keep the kitchen open and serve up The Colossal 24 hours a day. For every Miss Yoder, just remember there is also a Neil, a Nels, and a Mike out there who will encourage you. Find them. Bring them close. Work the relationship.

GROWING THE MOTOROLA RELATIONSHIP

Somewhere on the plane between Chicago and Dallas after my ego-deflating meeting with Motorola, I received some inspiration. I told myself we would continue to make better products and provide excellent service and support in order to keep The Genesis Group afloat during this transition. It would be difficult financially to forego this partnership with Motorola—and we'd have to be careful. But one thing was certain. The Genesis Group made the best product line in this field, and we knew it.

We would keep on doing good work—that's all I knew to do—with or without our biggest client. Our plan of approach was to market our services directly to potential customers. There was a little ramp up period, but we were able to eke out a living during this time.

Long story short, Motorola ended up buying our products again to replace the programs and products they had been cranking out in-house in the time we were apart. Large companies seem to have a common thread of being cyclical in nature. In this case, they once again figured out they were amazing at hardware and not so great at software. As Genesis kept plodding along, the cycle came back around to us. When we were finally back in business with Motorola, we had accumulated over 700 items that were selling in their parts catalogue throughout the world, including Latin America and Asia. The Genesis Group became a proud partner again with Motorola, simply because I refused to believe the lies I was hearing in my head. Therefore, I refused to quit.

I've conquered The Colossal more than once in my lifetime with a lot of help from my bride and friends. It's not a one-and-done kind of situation. You'll likely experience the pain of discouragement and rejection multiple times, personally and professionally. Remember that you eat a Failure Sandwich one bite at a time, even when it seems overwhelming. But you don't get through it alone. Let your friends and family pull up a chair and help you process it when times get really tough—which is exactly what was about to happen to me.

SIX

The Seven-Year Ick

In addition to being the name of a 1950s movie with Marilyn Monroe, the seven-year itch is a common belief that any kind of happiness heads downhill after seven years. I named this next Failure Sandwich The Seven-Year Ick. It's exactly what the name implies—something bad. It's the one dreaded thing you don't want to happen to you, and when it does, you think you'll never get through it. It can happen every seven years, or several times in one year.

I prayed as a young man for God to make me a millionaire for him. Around the same time that I was finally beginning to reach the level of success in business that I'd dreamed about, my pastor invited me and some other men to a Bible study called *Experiencing God*. The thing is, I did not experience God at all. Or, I should say, I did experience him but not in a way that I liked. It was as if I forgot to pay the water bill, and God shut off the water. Adding in the rest of my mental baggage, I wondered what stupid thing I did to turn off the communication faucet.

This study marked the start of another dark period spiritually that, according to the zippy marketing text on the back of the workbook, should have instead been the most amazing and inspiring time in my life. If God loved me so much, and was blessing my business, why didn't I feel as if he cared? Why did it seem as if he'd abandoned me?

I read the story of Job many times during that study. It's a book in the Old Testament about a man who loses everything that's important to him. He feels as if God is a million miles away, and I knew exactly what Job meant.

"God, where ARE you?" I asked time after time.

Nothing. Nada. No answer.

I still don't understand what happened back then (or why). But I'm okay with it now because I think God allowed me to go through that season in order to know this: You can get through anything, even if you don't understand why it's happening to you. When you commit yourself to God—when you commit yourself to anything, really— there are always ups and downs. There are periods of amazing faith where you know God is answering your prayers before your eyes. You cannot explain it any other way. And there are periods of silence, where you wonder if God is even with you.

When I later decided to lead some of my Genesis staff to do the same *Experiencing God* study, I gave them fair warning. "You may want to get up and leave right about now," I cautioned them on the first day we met. They just looked at me, bewildered. Then I explained about the trying experience I'd had when I went through the group study.

"If you're not prepared for God to challenge you," I told them, "it's really best to walk out now." I don't recall if anyone left, but I was dead serious!

The Seven-Year Ick is unique from other Failure Sandwiches because it usually involves a big change. Bad stuff happens in life and life changes forever. It's the unexpected left turn or an out-of-the-blue crushing blow that threatens to knock you completely off course.

It's tempting when you're facing The Seven-Year Ick to wonder, "Why is this awful thing happening to me? What have I done to deserve it?" You might sense self-doubt creeping in, making you feel like a flop. When life-altering change enters the picture—and it will, in a variety of forms and usually when you least expect it— your initial reaction to it generally affects your ability to deal with it long-term.

When life moves you from point A to point B, it's rarely done through joyous happenings but almost always with

problems and backward steps. My observations lead me
to believe that this maxim is as true for people of faith as
it is for the rest of the world. According to Jewish history,
it took 40 years for the Hebrews to make the relatively
short journey out of Egyptian slavery to the Promised
Land. Wouldn't that discourage you? Don't you know they
were frustrated? And yet, they were learning difficult but
valuable life lessons the entire time that they would end
up passing down through generations.

Instead of considering it a problem when your plans
go awry and The Seven-Year Ick lands in front of you,
think about this change in a different way. It might be the
very thing you need at the moment to help you see life
from a different perspective. Remember the condiments
you can add to make a Failure Sandwich taste better?
Patience. Prayer. And now you can add to that list
"perspective." What if the bad news you received can
lead you to something better? What if The Seven-Year Ick
wasn't meant to derail you but instead to redirect you?
Have you had Seven-Year Ick experiences and it's many
years down the road before perspective kicks in and you
realize how that "icky" event helped you?

I can still remember how much I wanted a CB radio
as a kid. But my father couldn't afford to buy me that, so
he bought us a kit for assembling walkie talkies instead.
It was NOT an easy task. We ended up having to ask my
cousin Bob, who was an electronics technician, to come
over and solder together the trickiest parts to make the

thing work. But I found more enjoyment in knowing the ins and outs of those walkie talkies than I ever could have gained from a pre-made CB radio. Looking back, I see that very clearly. But at the time, I was sure disappointed. Life rarely hands you what you want. You have to work for it. And you end up learning more that way than if everything came easily to you. It's all in how you look at things. Perspective is essential to dealing with The Seven-Year Ick.

COMBINING BUSINESS AND FAITH

People often ask me how I balance being a businessperson with also being a person of faith. There are several things at play, I tell them. Perspective is one way that doing business as a believer can differ from someone without a faith structure. For example, a believer and non-believer can wildly differ in their approach to The Seven-Year Ick when it involves conflict.

Two people in business who are both believers can pray for God to direct, to prosper, to protect, and to guide their companies and their lives. Both can work hard to be witnesses for God for the benefit of their employees, investors, and suppliers. Both can genuinely want to glorify and honor God in all that they do. But what if a business conflict arises between them? How should they deal with it?

If you're in conflict with someone you work with, stop looking for who is right and who is wrong for a moment and ask yourself, "Am I being moved to something else that life has in store?" If you remain solely caught up in untangling who did what when and why they did it, you may miss out on understanding the greater purpose surrounding WHY this conflict or crisis is even happening to you in the first place.

Not only that, but also there is a HIGH probability that God has a greater purpose in mind. He may be doing something for someone else whenever YOU run into problems. I tend to forget that and focus only on myself!

How about you? Have you looked around in the middle of a pity party to notice if you are part of a bigger plan that you have not yet been able to see? It's not always all about you—or me! Do I understand this concept fully? Nope. But I do know that if I try to fight against the greater purpose for my life and consequently ignore or even work against God's plan for others, it is the worst place in the world to be. In my prayer life, I regularly ask God to make me the best businessperson that I can be. I use that dreaded word "make." That means that I'm asking him to change, mold, and move me. If I'm asking him to do all of that, how can I be upset when change happens that I don't like at the moment? Notice the word "moment" and remember from our earlier discussion about time—that's what it is, a moment, considering the total years of your life.

There have definitely been times when I felt as if God was speaking directly to me during the most painful phases of my life. It was as if he said, *"If you are praying for ME to REALLY do all that you ask, and you are praying for MY will to be done... then you better be ready to accept it, no matter what that is. EVEN if it is painful. Are you prepared to be moved?"*

It might as well have been an audible voice from heaven, although it never has been. Whenever I felt that I was being moved to something different ("better" is implied here if we are asking God for the very best options possible), there was always heartache attached. No way around it. If you want something better for your life, there is almost always pain involved.

As you raise children, there is a 100% chance that you want the best for them. But that doesn't mean you let them do whatever they want. What they think is best, especially when they are young, is rarely what you know is best. Why? Because you have been there, done that. You know from your experience that if they continue down a particular path, they will ultimately fail, or at least not meet their potential. So you push your children, making them uncomfortable and cranky and angry with you. Do you think God's relationship with you might be exactly the same?

A WATCHING WORLD

And one more thing. If you are going through The Seven-Year Ick, remember that others are watching you throughout the process to see how you handle it—

especially if you claim to be a person of faith. People who look up to you are observing your responses to your biggest problems. Right now, it may not be easy, but do your best to keep focused on what's bigger and better down the road. Popular culture has a term for this practice of paying attention to the way things look to outsiders: "optics." It's simply focusing on the bigger picture, which in my case, happens to be whatever God is up to in this world. I call it "kingdom optics"—the plans and priorities he has for me.

So, if you're a believer, I have a question for you. What does your everyday behavior and kneejerk reaction to what life throws your way say to others about who God is and what he's up to in the world? What are the kingdom optics? You can do or say something that in your mind is perfectly fine, but what does it say to someone else? How does it look to someone else who is not a believer?

I grew up in a conservative culture where people made the choices simple. They said you couldn't "drink, smoke, chew, or go with girls who do." My parents wouldn't even let me go to movies when I was a kid! My mother knew I wouldn't reject MY faith if I went to a Hollywood movie, but she was concerned someone else might stumble in their faith.

Social mores have changed—and I go to movies today, by the way—but the principle my mom practiced still holds true. When I post something on my personal Facebook page, for example, I try to look at the optics of the message I'm passing on and think through how this might look to someone else. I'm a leader, and leaders are held to higher standards.

I keep a letter in my drawer written by a former employee over 20 years ago. She didn't pull any punches— she named some specific actions of mine that she felt, as a Christian businessperson, did not honor God. Honestly, before this letter, I thought I was doing pretty well. I'm not perfect by a long shot, but sheez? Nevertheless, she called me out—and it wasn't fun. That said, I also knew without a doubt that the letter was written with a humble spirit of genuinely wanting to help me as a person, not to tear me down.

Leaders tell others, "Follow me, and I'll lead the way." Now, it may be off a cliff, but just issuing this statement holds me accountable to walk carefully. If I tell someone to watch what I do as a model, that holds me to a higher standard. I can't go out and be reckless with my attitudes and actions. It puts pressure on me, and I have to be willing to receive others' opinions on how I'm doing.

As a relatively young CEO, I was more likely to crater under criticism. Now I've been in this position long enough to know that I won't do everything 100% right. I do a lot of things wrong; and I'm having some success. But the scale says I'm probably doing better than 50% of the right things.

One day at our church choir rehearsal, an older choir member pulled me aside and said that she had been praying for me. She said she felt led to tell me, "God has favored you." That's heavy. That word encouraged me so much, but it came with a responsibility. If that's true, I need to tune my life so I can watch and listen for the times God wants to get my attention so I can maximize HOW God has favored me.

From time to time, I still open my desk drawer and read the letter my former employee wrote as a reminder that people are watching me, and I am accountable to others for my behavior—even and especially in the little things.

"IF ONLY..." AND OTHER LIES WE TELL OURSELVES

Nothing ever stays the same. No matter how much we might hate change, no job is the perfect job, and no place in life is the perfect place. Life moves us along, and when that happens, your perspective of WHERE you are must also change. Start envisioning yourself doing and experiencing whatever's next, long before you get to that point. Don't get stuck on insisting that you get to keep doing what you're doing right now and being where you are at this moment. Problems are an opportunity to take stock and see where you could be going NEXT with different eyes. The Seven-Year Ick is your chance to be open to what might happen in the future.

I've actually been accused of being the agent of doom when I had the unfortunate job as the owner of a company to serve The Seven-Year Ick to someone. I've had to help someone transition to another opportunity because they're not a good fit with Genesis. And I've also been guilty of looking at people and situations the same way when it seemed something unfair was happening to me. Sometimes agents of change are merely dressed up to *look* like agents of doom. Kind of like the "blue dress vs. gold dress" Internet debate of years past, maybe the longer you look, the clearer the purpose will become.

It's easy to point to outside influences and think they are what's ruining your life. It's natural to think life would be perfect, "If ONLY this person behaved better..." or "If ONLY this or that would happen or would *not* have happened..." Fill in the blank however you want. You can choose to embrace the idea that this particular crisis is happening to PREPARE you and motivate you to pursue something new or different down the road.

That was the case with Genesis in the late Nineties. We were making great strides as a company, fueling our passion every day and creating just shy of bleeding edge technology, much of which was used to support public safety. But it didn't mean we weren't making mistakes along the way, like we almost did in the next story.

DID THAT REALLY ALMOST HAPPEN?

In 1998 a businessman I knew through some connections contacted me with an idea. He was looking for a way to make inexpensive phone calls overseas. An engineer had created a prototype "box" that could route calls through the Internet and then inexpensively tie into the local phone system anywhere in the world. The engineer was good at hardware development, but he had no idea how to market and make money with the idea. This story took place before services like Skype and WhatsApp offered free Wi-Fi phone calling that now connects our world through the Internet.

The box did not have a name, so I named it IDA. It stood for Internet Digital Appliance, and we named the company IDATel. IDA was so simple that even Grandma could use it, which is exactly what we depicted in our marketing. Grandma could talk to her grandson who was studying overseas just by hitting *22 before the international number, and IDA did the rest. It dialed up Grandma's local ISP (Internet Service Provider) using the dial-up modems of that day. The call traveled very inexpensively over the ocean via the Internet, and then it jumped into the local phone system of the country she was calling. Voila! Grandma and her grandson were talking without breaking the bank!

The technology used what were called gateways, which allowed telephone communications to be hauled across the Internet dirt cheap and then plugged into the local phone system for the actual call. We figured out we could make a profit and charge just 30 cents a minute in a time when a regular international phone call ranged from seven to twelve dollars a minute!

I wrote all our marketing materials as well as the

training manual for IDATel. We had very little capital, but our initial success skyrocketed in Barbados and other international destinations. We even shelled out some cash and placed an ad for IDATel in the *American Way* magazine for American Airlines, hoping to target business customers and the public.

One day my business partner received a phone call from a group of businessmen in Pakistan who had seen the *American Way* ad for IDATel. They wanted a test unit. Afterward, they extended an invitation for five of our guys to fly over to Pakistan to discuss a larger order of 30 units.

After negotiations, our team flew over with 30 units in their luggage for the grand opening of IDATel Pakistan in the early spring of 2000. The grandeur of that event was followed by an 18-hour journey by train with the Pakistani business leaders to demonstrate IDA to their "investors." After a while, the train stopped at an isolated station in the middle of nowhere. A local worker appeared from the train station dragging a long telephone cord that was then connected to IDA in one of the rail cars.

Our team was told they needed to wait for their investors to arrive so that they could make a few test calls. Hours later, a cloud of dust appeared on the horizon as five men on horseback crested a hill and tied up their horses to the train as my team members watched wide-eyed. Once inside, this new group of Pakistani men made a series of phone calls on IDA to what my team understood to be their hotel groups in the USA.

The Pakistani investors were very pleased with the device, including the bonus 128-bit encryption we had built into IDA that made every call extremely secure. To the amazement of our team, the investors and Pakistani business leaders announced that they wanted to place an order for a container-load of devices before the beginning of 2001.

My team came home to the USA elated about the staggering $10,000,000 order, although the way the meeting went down was one for the record books. We set about trying to raise the $10,000,000 we needed to build thousands of IDA units and set up the larger infrastructure to handle the blossoming business. Translation: we were in a panic. We did presentations in Dallas, Austin, New York, and Los Angeles trying to raise the needed capital. But it was never going to happen. I had to close IDATel in November 2000 for several reasons, including the lack of funding to fulfil this huge order.

You haven't heard the craziest part of this story yet. In the fall of 2001, 9/11 happened, and our team learned a word at the very same time that the rest of the USA and the world learned it: the Taliban. Remember those Pakistani "investors" on horseback? They were, in fact, members of the Taliban—although that word did not exist in our vocabulary back then when the world was much more innocent than it is now. At the time, we naively thought "taliban" meant nomads on horseback. Looking back, we can only assume that they may have been planning to use our device to make encrypted phone calls to their operatives stationed all over the world.

As I said, IDATel failed for a lot of reasons, although this order that thankfully failed to materialize was NOT one of them. I lost nearly a half-million dollars I had invested, along with credibility and precious time. The lesson in this story is to embrace failure when it happens—it can teach you so much and even save you from doing something foolish. In fact, that IDATel loss actually set the stage for other great things to come (more on that in the next chapter). So be careful not to wallow in loss as a bad thing. Sure, it hurts, but let my story help you envision past the hurt and see what good *might*come from it. The Seven-Year Ick may not be so icky after all.

GET PAST THE TRUCK

The first time I merged onto an Interstate highway on my Can-Am Spyder RT, I was gripping the handlebars so tightly that my knuckles were white. Bobbie was riding behind me, and she can tell you we were both chock full of adrenaline as we headed west on Interstate 20 into the sunset that night. When I passed my first 18-wheeler, we were buffeted by such a strong wind that I truly thought it was the end of the line.

"We're going to die! We're going to DIE!" I kept thinking as I pulled alongside the truck at 70 mph.

And you know what? We got past the truck. And we didn't die.

"So, that's how you do that," I remember thinking to myself when we were safely down the road. I later learned about Spyder suspension and stronger-than-factory stabilizer bars. Once I upgraded those changes, it made for a more stable ride.

An almost-fail taught me some things I didn't know before. As I was being buffeted by that truck, if I gave up and decided it was all over anyway, I might have made a rash move that killed both of us. But instead I kept our motorcycle on a straight a path as I could manage, gave it more throttle, and moved ahead of the truck to safety.

The next time I passed a truck, I released a little more of my death grip on the handlebars. And I realized something else. The buffeting wind that pushes you one way also brings you back to center. Failure, or even the threat of it, will do that for you much of the time. The more hammered you are by failure, the more you will pay attention and learn from it.

When failure is buffeting you, you will eventually learn that you aren't likely to die because of it. Loosen your grip and just pass on through the trial to the other side. Learn something and say to yourself, "So, *that's* how you get through this." Failure teaches you to loosen your grips on the handlebars of life when you're passing an 18-wheeler-size problem. You'll get pummeled by the wind, but you *will* get past the truck. And it won't be quite so scary the next time. You might even find yourself having a little fun.

NO TIME TO SELL

Genesis kept moving along during this period of my life where changes were happening at a rapid rate. We were adding staff and refining our product line all the time. I killed off my bestselling EZBill software sometime around 2005 because it was in my customers' best interest to do so. We weren't providing technical support with the product any longer. Second, there were newer replacements on the market. Still, some of my customers were disappointed when we killed EZBill because it was so darn simple to use. But for me, the decision was based on the Mack Truck Problem—again, if something happened to me, no one could help a customer out of a hole. Over 15 years later, the phone occasionally still rings with a question about EZBill, and the caller sometimes gets routed to my desk! The problem is that I've forgotten more than I remember about it!

Sure, I had a few opportunities to sell EZBill software to investors early on and make a healthy profit. And that would have been that. But I was happy to plod along and let the company grow and diversify slowly into whatever shape and size it was meant to be. In fact, there were two big opportunities to sell Genesis as a whole early on, but it was in the best interest of the company to turn them down.

Those who wanted to buy us could not (or maybe "would not" is closer to the truth) uphold the culture that our leadership team worked so hard to create. They did not assure me they would value the people I'd had a hand in developing and who had a hand in growing Genesis for many years. At Genesis, we host baby showers and attend funerals. When a teenager of one of our employees graduates from high school, we give him or her a laptop to help with college. Something as small as Genesis paying for car repairs for a valuable employee goes a long way to underscore how much a company truly cares. The people and our culture were two non-negotiables that never quite made it to the top of the Letter of Intent I received from potential buyers. For me, it was a non-starter.

I am also glad I did not sell the company because there was a lot more waiting to be written in this story. Lots of changes—and not just in the area of business.

AGING PARENTS – THE CHANGE EVERYONE MUST FACE

One of my most difficult personal experiences with the changes associated with The Seven-Year Ick was the death of my father. My dad was one of the most gracious and wise people I've ever known. His brain was sharp, but his body gave out at 92 years of age. My father once told me that the good thing about being alert at 92 is that you know everything going on around you. The bad thing is that you know everything going on around you!

Growing up, I was much closer to my mom than my dad simply because my dad was always working. When he retired, he and my mom moved to Longview, Texas, where I'd gone to school so they could be near us in East Texas as they both advanced in age.

My mom died of ovarian cancer just before Christmas in 2001. Dad called me when she died, and I rushed to the hospital room where her body lay. Dad put it so well when he said through sobs, "Phil, that's not Mom. It's only her leftover body. We'll see her soon in Heaven." I remember deliberately taking a different route home from the hospital that day to get my thoughts together. On the way to my house, and over the next few days, I relived memories.

From my earliest memory, my mom helped me get to school and to church, fixed my scrapes and sunburns, and made sure I did my homework. She was my cheering section at school plays and took me fishing just once (it was a disaster!). Mom was my Google, dictionary, and spell check. More than once, my mom used my dad as leverage whenever I'd done something wrong at home. "Just wait until your father gets home!" she'd warn me.

I don't think I necessarily favor one of my parents more than the other. I can see in myself both the fastidiousness, detail-oriented nature of my mom and the creative side of my dad. They were perfect partners in everything. For example, I have tremendous memories of seeing Dad and Mom performing together, singing country music

Phil Burks

and gospel duets. My dad liked to say that when he "got saved" his guitar got saved also. I went along whenever they were invited to different gatherings to perform country songs, including "Tumbling Tumble Weeds" by the Sons of the Pioneers and other hits.

True to my dad's nature, they'd always take a break halfway in the show and transition into what he called "sacred" music. The band would take off their Western hats and perform some gospel songs as part of their closing program. One day when I was about 12 years old I heard them rehearsing an old Gaither tune standing side by side at a music stand in our living room in Pennsylvania. My dad sang lead and mom sang alto. I walked in quietly and casually started humming a third part in harmony while playing with a toy on the floor. My dad stopped mid-tune, wide-eyed, and said, "Come up here, boy! We'll make this a trio." I moved from my seat in the audience to the stage that day, which marked my introduction to singing at church and special events alongside my parents.

Consequently, I never have stage fright. To this day, I would much rather be in front of a large group of people speaking or singing than be in a group of people making small talk. Put me at a table of people I don't know and I become a wallflower. But put me up front to sing or speak on an area where I'm the subject matter expert, and I become a whole other person who is comfortable in his own skin.

My father was lonely after my mom died. When widowers pop up on the radar, the casseroles come out. My dad was no exception to this tradition started by lovely widows seeking male companionship. A few months before his 80th birthday, he told me he was thinking of getting married again. I gave him my blessing, and he was grateful.

"I wanted to tell you about this before I turned 80 next month," he added. "Because it sure sounds better getting married again at 79 than it does at 80!" Dad married a wonderful woman named Edith. I served as his best man and sang at their wedding. Edith and Dad spent many years together before she quietly died one Saturday morning at home of a brain hemorrhage.

With Bobbie's amazing help and leadership, we eventually moved my father to an assisted living facility in Tyler, where he and I spent more time together than ever. Over time, his care needs increased, and I made sure I talked with him virtually every day because I sensed time was growing short. He wasn't a fan of nursing homes— and neither was I. But assisted living, he did not mind. My dad made friends there, and I took my laptop with me on lazy Saturday afternoon visits to show him Google Earth images of where we used to live in Levittown and even where he grew up in Virginia. "Oh, my..." he'd marvel in his Deep South accent as we flew around the world from his little room.

We talked through tough times that he and I'd had

over the years, and we revisited so many good memories. I am so glad we rehearsed those times because I might have forgotten the details. I have a fear of forgetting—the little and the big things. One of my most embarrassing moments was when I was singing in a quartet at our church and flubbed one of my lines. I remember looking up at the "confidence monitor" on the back wall of the auditorium that displays the lyrics for just such an occasion. But the words may as well have been in Chinese. For the next measure, I literally sang—in tune— "Blah, blah, blah, blah..." I have a fear of forgetting.

My wife, on the other hand, has the blessing and curse of not being able to forget anything. I can ask her when such and such happened with so and so and she remembers. How does she recall that stuff?

I want my kids to know me. Toward that end, I keep a file I call, "Important Things in Phil's Life" and I write simple phrases and even one-word triggers of special milestones in my business and personal life.

I can attend a meeting and not take a single note—and then afterward compose a detailed email about goals and assign tasks to specific people. That, I can remember. But I fear forgetting all the important stuff that makes for good memories and composes the tapestry of a life. That's why I recommend this practice of writing down milestones, good and bad. I try to be conservative and concise in what I write. Make it as simple as possible. Don't get complicated about it. Jot down the event and what you can remember about it, using at least two or three of your five senses. Then one day you'll have memories you can share with others when all you have is time on your hands.

"You're paying too much for this," my dad said one day, referring to the bill at the assisted living facility. Bobbie and I had always planned to take care of my father this way, and he and I talked about it for the first time that afternoon. My father had never talked about money with me after I became an adult. I remember one time as a teenager when I made a snarky comment about our middle-class standing, and he said, "Son, I'll have you know that I could buy a Cadillac this moment for all cash." And that's about all I ever knew about our family finances. Likewise, I never talked to my dad about how well our business was doing, although he kept up with me and was always interested in what I was doing at work.

"Dad, remember when you told me you could buy a Cadillac for cash?" I asked my dad when he told me how worried he was that I was having to pay for his care. He shook his head and smiled.

"Well, Dad," I said, "God's been good to me. You might say I could buy a Cadillac dealership if I wanted to!"

He laughed, and I laughed back before he stuck out his hand and said, "Shake my hand then. I always wanted to shake the hand of a millionaire!"

Eventually, my dad moved to hospice care. Bobbie

and I would visit him most every afternoon after work to talk, sing a little, and pray. As the wintry January days went along and his time drew closer to the end, we increased our visits. In his final couple of weeks, Bobbie and I ended up doing all the talking, singing, and praying. Some of us have the blessing of knowing when we or our loved ones are going to die. I remember my dad joking, "If I'd known I was going to live to 92, I would have taken much better care of myself." He had a point. But none of us knows how much time is left on the clock. If I had a choice, I'd like to know the day I'll die. I'd have the chance to wrap it up and say some final words to the people I love. I'm forever grateful that Dad and I had the chance to do that.

I walked out of his room at hospice care one day and was almost to the door when he said in a raspy half-whisper, "Hey, Phil!"

"Yeah, Dad?" I asked.

"You got a gun?"

I froze. "Dad, why do you want a gun?"

He nodded at the clock hanging on the wall in front of his bed and said, "I want to shoot the clock on that wall. It sure is running slow."

I laughed. "You still got it, Dad," I thought to myself as I told him goodbye and closed his door.

The number one thing on my mind as Dad was dying in hospice was how I was going to teach my kids about how to do dying and death. They are two different things.

I am not afraid of death, but I'm afraid of dying. When my time comes, I want my children to have seen death for what it is and to know you can do it without panic, but with grace. If you believe there's something more, as hard as that concept is to grasp, it's not a horrible thing when your loved one dies. They're just changing addresses.

What I'm writing about in this book is similar to something I learned from someone else. *SCRUM* by Jeff Sutherland is one of my favorite business books, and it's required reading at Genesis. I have always tended to break life down into bite-sized, manageable chunks. Jeff teaches you in his book about how to increase your productivity by tackling seemingly insurmountable problems one step at a time. Hospice care is a wonderful organization that helps families understand what happens to the body when death approaches. When I broke the reality of my dad's death into daily, then hourly pieces, I could handle it. I wasn't sad necessarily, but I could face it and tell myself, "Okay, this is really happening."

Death is the ultimate Big Nasty, and it's the unwelcome thing that comes to all of our families at some point in life. The truth is that 100% of us will experience it. When life serves up this doozy on the menu regarding someone you love, it's not something you can take in at one sitting. Sometimes it takes the rest of your life to process it.

Ask anyone who believes in the eternal life that's promised in John 3:16 if they would come back from Heaven to Earth. They would blow a raspberry and say, "No way." To ask my father to stick around for my pleasure would have been selfish on my part. More than once as he would drift in and out of a non-communicative state, I would whisper, "It's okay, Dad. You can go home." It was better to go on to the next place, which for him was Heaven, and on January 20, 2009, that's exactly what he did.

SEVEN

The Looky Loo

When I was going through some old photo albums, I found a picture of me standing next to a 100,000-volt Tesla Coil I built in Dad's workshop in 1966. I was almost 14 years old. I'd found a description of how to build the contraption in a *Popular Electronics* magazine. The parts list called for a neon sign transformer, glass, metal, a spark gap, and a HUGE coil of thin wire. Mom drove me all over to find the parts, including the glass, and I set about building a jig to create the giant coil and all the other components.

Early experiments showed that I needed more glass to build bigger capacitors. Dad had taken out our winter storm windows from our house, and they were the perfect size! You know the old axiom about how sometimes asking for forgiveness is easier than asking for permission? I "borrowed" two of our window panes and THEN told Mom and Dad what I had done. They were not too happy, but they let it go since they could see my passion for making this project a success.

Without my parents' knowledge, one night I took my final creation upstairs to my bedroom and fired it up! Our neighbor rushed over and began pounding on our front door yelling about a fire he'd just seen in the upstairs window. My dad ran to my room to see what was going on and then spent the next few minutes calmly explaining to the frazzled neighbor that it was just his son pretending to be an electrical scientist. I was the happiest kid on the whole block that night. My parents could have grounded me for life—but they didn't.

One of the biggest mistakes you can make as a leader is squelching someone else's passion. Especially after they take a big chance, and even more so after they take a big chance and mess up! Failure and disappointment will zap someone else's passion like lightning hitting a transformer. Their dreams go dead in an instant. Your job as a leader, parent, coach, pastor—whatever—is not to let that happen to the good people under your care. That's why this chapter shares what I've learned about dealing with OTHER people's failures and mistakes. What can you do to keep THEIR passion alive when they fail? How can you help them recover from failure—and where do you draw the line?

I call this particular Failure Sandwich The Looky Loo because people love to pass judgment on someone else's mistakes. It's why traffic slows when there's a fender bender on the shoulder of the road—everyone wants to take a long look! Don't be that guy—The Looky Loo—the one who watches someone else fail and even enjoys it to some degree. In business, keep someone's passion alive and help them over the hump, while maintaining your own convictions about what's best for your company. In life, be someone's encourager.

WHAT IS PASSION?

First, let's talk about passion. I will spend time with someone who shows potential and passion when the going gets rough. People without passion are just putting in the time and going home at the end of the day, that's all. That's one of the reasons why we don't hire strictly for intelligence at The Genesis Group. Patrick Lencioni, a business expert and author of several books, says to look for someone who is "hungry, humble, and smart." As I look back over the years when I was hiring folks, I applied that principle without knowing that was what I was doing. I was always much more interested in the person and what drives them than I was impressed by their education.

I tell people all the time that my BSEET degree from LeTourneau University simply proved that I could begin and end a difficult task without quitting! It has nothing to do with how smart (or not) I am. It's ALL important regarding job candidates, but I felt I could teach a person the mechanics of coding if they possessed the desire and basic aptitude.

One of my favorite questions for potential employees was about their hobbies. I wanted to see if the candidate was creative, self-starting, and curious. These traits are not on a résumé; they are indications of something deeper because they represent a person's character. They get at the core values that drive someone's passion. If you are passionate and want to do good work in the world, you'll find you can go forward, even when you have a bad season and need to retool. Being hungry, humble, and smart will PUSH you forward.

Where do you develop a particular passion? I believe passion is modeled for you. You may have a propensity toward many things—but someone modeling a behavior amplifies your propensities. Here's a negative example. Alcoholism is a propensity that may run in your family. If your immediate family models it for you day after day, you may develop an unwanted passion for alcohol.

On the other hand, my dad modeled something positive that I've kept with me my whole life. He showed up at work every day to maintain his livelihood. He was also a creative woodworker at heart who invented ideas in his spare time. He even submitted some of his ideas at US Steel where he worked. Over the years he earned cash awards for saving time and costs, while increasing production. But the money didn't matter to him. It was the passion of creating something that motivated him. What my dad's passion did for me personally meant more than money. He let me come alongside him in his workshop as he worked and modeled for me what it looked like to love what you do and enjoy hard work. I need to mention that it never was a classroom-type setting between Dad and myself. I only listened and watched as he worked. Remember that your employees are also doing the same. The Looky Loo has more than one meaning here.

FINDING BERNIE MAY AFTER 55 YEARS

My mentor Bernie May is one of the most passionate individuals I've ever met in my life. He is in his eighties and currently keeps busy working out a written plan of what God wants him to accomplish until he reaches 90. He served as the former CEO of Wycliffe Bible Translators. Wycliffe, if you didn't know, was founded in 1942 and is the largest Bible translation organization in the world today. Bernie was also the founder of Seed Company, an organization that partners donors with worldwide Bible translation projects.

Bible translation is pretty high tech these days. There are hundreds of missionaries around the world like my friend Ross, who came to me in the mid-Nineties needing a computer program to translate the Bible from the Chichewa language into a parallel English Chichewa

Bible. I connected Ross with Greg, one of our Genesis programmers, who took the next two years to write the program in between his work duties. This is the kind of high-tech work Wycliffe and Seed Company is doing today and so much more.

As mentioned earlier, I first knew Bernie decades ago as a friend of my mom and dad since they were about the same age. Bernie was a young missionary pilot for JAARS (Jungle Aviation And Radio Service). JAARS was founded in 1948 by Cameron Townsend (also the founder of Wycliffe) because, in Townsend's words, "Airplanes and radios don't just make translation easier; they make it possible." For over 60 years, JAARS has been piloting equipment to set up radios in random rainforests and to install satellite uplinks in barren deserts to translate the Bible in foreign tongues in some of the remotest places on Earth.

I remember Bernie took me for my first ride in an airplane as a young child. To a curious kid growing up thousands of miles away from any jungle, meeting a real-life missionary pilot in radio work was like meeting an astronaut. I never forgot Bernie, although I lost touch with him for many years.

One day when I was in my early sixties, I started thinking about Bernie after a development director for a Tyler Christian radio network was talking about Seed Company. My dad had long since died, and I wondered if it were even possible that the pilot I knew as a boy who was so instrumental in my life was still alive. I fired up my computer and began one of my research treks.

I came across a Bernie May who had served as the head of Wycliffe and was now busy in the latter part of his life directing Seed Company. Was this the same Bernie May? If so, it would be an even greater coincidence because my church had been partnering with Seed Company for many years. Several people in our church had even sponsored the translation of the Book of John into a foreign language.

First I have no idea if this email is getting to the right Bernie May...I'm wondering if you are, in fact, the Bernie May that had a hand in a cascade of events in my life?

This is how I began an email to the Bernie May listed at Seed Company's address. I recalled my parents and how I grew up in Pennsylvania, yada yada. Then I sent my note into cyberspace to see if there was a connection to be made.

At 3:30 in the afternoon not long afterward I received the answer I'd been hoping for. Sitting in my inbox was an email from Bernie! He wrote:

Dear Phil,
Yes, I am that Bernie May, and your folks played a significant part in my life and ministry.

Your dad was someone I greatly admired and a real friend. He encouraged me when I was just getting started in the formidable years of my faith journey. And I have more to the story that likely you don't know.

Bernie and I quickly worked out a plan for Bernie to fly his single-engine Moony airplane to Tyler Pounds Field airport to meet up with me.

DON'T GIVE UP ON SOMEONE

We had a wonderful 90-minute reunion when he flew to Tyler that day, and we reminisced about God's work in our lives. Bernie was even able to shed a lot of light on my dad's time in prison, something my father never talked about with me after that one day at his house when he first shared the revelation.

I learned that Bernie grew up in one of the roughest neighborhoods bordering Philadelphia in a town called Marcus Hook. Bernie's dad was a teenage alcoholic, and his mom was only 14. After Bernie was born, his parents decided to start over and began attending Marcus Hook Baptist Church where my grandparents, Roscoe and Maude Eastwood, also attended. The young Mays soon asked Jesus to be Lord of their lives and along the way made friends with a single woman who would one day become my mother, Dorothy Eastwood.

The Mays and Dorothy were involved in their church's

prison ministry. Bernie joked that the church led a prison ministry because in this rough area of town, many church members' friends were behind bars. The prison ministry was the only way they could see them! While my dad was serving time, he attended song services and listened to the speakers from Bernie's church talk about the Gospel.

Bernie told me that they began praying specifically for my dad to become a Christian. After my dad became a believer, Bernie said they prayed for him to be released early by the parole board, which they did. This led to my dad meeting and marrying my mom, which led to me!

Bernie and his parents knew what to do with The Looky Loo. They could have easily pointed at my dad and said, "Hey, you made your bed. Now lie in it." Bernie and his parents could have given up on my dad and written him off as a hopeless man who made a mistake.

But the May family saw something in my dad, despite the failures in his past, and that vision gave my dad (and me) a different future. "The boundary lines for you have fallen in pleasant places, you have a great inheritance," noted Bernie in one of his emails to me, quoting a verse from Psalms. Bobbie has a similar saying on a plaque in her office that reads: "Coincidence is when God works a miracle and decides to remain anonymous."

My mom and dad supported Bernie when he was a young missionary requiring $98 a month to live and do his work. I think my parents gave him $25 a month toward that sum—a lot of money back in those days for a

steel worker. But they believed in what Bernie was doing
to help others. He was out there doing what they could
never do. Bobbie and I follow in my parents' footsteps
and have the pleasure of supporting many missionaries
and ministries today. It's the fulfillment of what I learned
as a young adult about not BEING a missionary but
SENDING missionaries and SUPPORTING them.

I always credit Bernie for being an example of a life
committed to a cause that was greater than him. When
the Museum of the Bible opened in Washington D.C., one
of the exhibits was a wall full of Bibles that have been
translated into other languages. Under Bernie's watch,
missionaries and others have translated the Bible into
over 1800 various languages throughout the world. That
is passion in action.

Like Bernie, if you're passionate about something,
there's nothing you won't do to sacrifice for it. It will take
your energy and time, but in the end, you'll be glad you
did it. That's part of what it means to be successful.

I am as passionate about what I do as I ever have
been. And I am certain regarding my calling, but that
wasn't the case for much of my life. A person's calling will
morph as you gain more life experience. It may change
over time, but your passion usually remains tied to a
similar calling and a similar destination. You evolve as
time goes by, and so does your life's purpose.

At this point in my career, I'm totally clear in what
I'm to do with the time remaining. Fundamentally, my

calling has been and will continue to be enabling others to be and do better. That sounds noble enough. But it also means I may find myself knee-deep in the mud to help pull others out of a ditch when they do something wrong. Remember, The Looky Loo makes you point the finger and say, "Look at what you did wrong." Instead, I want to help others when things go awry.

WHEN PEOPLE MAKE MISTAKES

Passionate people build a good company by trial and error. They're going to make mistakes. What you do with those mistakes as a leader makes all the difference. Business guru Zig Ziglar always instructed leaders to "build the people," and then the people will build the company. I've seen this principle work. In the early days of Genesis, I tried to build people and let them construct the economy of what we're called to do. Today we've formalized that process. Graduates of the "Genesis School of Business and Leadership" spend eight weeks in a combination of formal and informal training as we give them the tools to become better leaders. We began with our senior leaders and filtered down to several other team members. We have tied into a formal process with Dave Anderson based on his book, *Becoming a Leader of Character*. Our team is given exercises within the Genesis work ecosystem to practice what they have learned.

Frustration comes as a leader when you push someone toward greatness, and they resist it. Be careful, parents, when this happens with your kids. Be mindful, managers, when your best people don't rise to the occasion in every instance. Sometimes you'll see a 180-degree turnaround in a person's performance. More often than not, a solid 45 degrees is good enough for now.

I'm okay with incremental change, and I'm very familiar with "little by little" as a concept. Little by little is how I built my business and my professional reputation. It's how I grew as a businessman, and it's what I look for and expect in others. One step at a time is the way we grow in influence, increase our level of expertise, and earn more responsibility. It's not the big steps and huge turnarounds that count in life as much as it is those small, 15-degree turns that end up pointing us in the right direction eventually. I want that 180-degree turn, but it might take several shifts and adjustments—stops and starts—to get someone to face a new direction and move forward. Leadership done right takes time.

Being overly gracious, however, will mess you up when it comes to business. I have a soft heart, and it gets me in trouble. A high level of sensitivity has landed me in hot water in the past. I have been told I'm overly gracious when someone makes a mistake. "How could a person be overly gracious?" I wanted to say the first time this came up. Isn't that a good thing?

What it translates to is that I have accepted a lot of behaviors and situations that I should not have condoned. The reason I did so is often because I irrationally believed I could fix it or change it by sheer willpower. Passion is not enough. Performance counts, too. You must be patient with others, while also drawing a firm line where your employees know that certain behavior is unacceptable. I was blind to this principle early on in business, and even more recently when I erroneously thought I could help fix the issue and "mentor" a person out of bad behavior. I thought I could somehow make it right and even believed that was my responsibility as CEO. I worked hard at changing this person, but I failed.

I think the best of people—I always do. It takes a long time to prove to me that you're *not* doing your best. I have learned to gather other people around me to help point out when someone crosses a line. You can extend TOO much grace in business, when you should not be as gracious. And if you find yourself being a person who tends to be full of grace, you need to surround yourself with advisors who are a little tougher and maybe not as emotionally invested with an employee or an investor.

I'm not totally cured. I can still let my warm and fuzzy emotions toward the person who is screwing up override the advice I receive.

If you have employees, you must realize that each one is his own person. Free will is a real thing, and people acting as their own moral agents can choose not to accept what leadership is telling them to do. You can let a gross violation of company policy go on way too long, and it ends up harming your culture. But there is also room for grace—there must be—when a good employee messes up and really needs a lesson in mercy more than a pink slip. I learned this lesson through an incident in my family that I've never forgotten.

GRACE IS ENOUGH

My youngest child was seven years old at summer camp when I received a phone call that made my blood run cold. The camp director was on the other line saying my son had been involved in an accident. "He's okay," she said, "and so is the other kid."

I felt my breath quicken, and the bottom dropped out of my stomach as she explained what happened. Josh and another kid had been in a group taking BB-gun instruction from a camp counselor who was showing them how to safely shoot at a row of aluminum cans. Josh picked up a gun and immediately pointed it in a joking way toward the kid's head. Fortunately, the counselor in charge pushed the gun away in time to avoid what could have been a terrible accident. The director was calling to tell me to come get Josh because they could no longer have him out there.

I was so angry and embarrassed. I flew out to the lake property, threw the car in park, and grabbed Josh to haul him across camp to our car. I struggled with a temper when I was a young man, and one time even punched a hole in a wall with my fist. The thing is, I was always mad at myself and never at another human being. I would become enraged with shame and disappointment whenever I made a mistake or did something wrong. My temper was a shameful secret I kept, and I didn't want anyone to know I had a problem in this area.

Now I was a grown man yelling at my son. I was terrified, truth be told, because he had come so close to causing irreparable damage to someone else and also ruining his future in the process.

"I was just goofing around, Dad," my son pleaded. "I wasn't going to pull the trigger."

I knew that. But what if someone had bumped his arm? What if? In an instant, anything could have happened. He was sorry he'd had to leave camp, but not really understanding what he'd done.

When we got home, we went into his room and I explained to him in a much calmer voice that I wanted him to feel the pain of the other child involved if the gun had fired. I pointed my finger to his head and described what it might have felt like for a hot pellet to enter his forehead. "What if you could no longer stand up?" I asked him. "What if you hit the ground and everything went dark? What if you suddenly lost control of all your bodily functions? Can you feel that, Josh? Can you?"

My breath quickened and my heart was pounding out of my chest when tears came to my son's eyes. I felt we were making progress and that the message was sinking in. I wanted Josh to experience fully the consequences he'd so narrowly avoided.

"You have to be punished for this, Josh. I know it was a mistake, but you must remember how bad this could have been." I asked him to lean over the bed and took a short wooden stick in hand. In my day, my parents applied the "trouble stick" to the seat of the problem and in my case, it worked.

Josh was crying at this point. I was crying. I could barely see Josh through a blur of tears, but I could hear his sobs of fear and grief. And every time I tell this story I cry because it is so burned into my mind. I was still angry and planned on spanking him, but at the last second I prayed and asked God, "What should I do?"

This was my only son. We'd almost lost him at birth in a medical emergency when he was only hours old. My wife had cried gut-wrenching sobs as the nurses wheeled him away in his isolette incubator to board a careflight to a Dallas NICU. I'd driven like a madman two hours to meet the helicopter. For a week, I sang to our baby nearly constantly until the day we could finally take him home for the first time.

Fast-forward back to this moment in his room. It took all my strength to raise the paddle high over my head to punish my child. And then, without thinking and in a split second, I slapped the paddle on the bed with a thunderous whack!

My son winced at the sound. He looked over at me, his eyes as wide as saucers. Had I missed?

"Josh...this is a lesson in grace." I choked out the

words, surprised at how easily they came, although I had not planned on saying them until that very moment. "I want you to know Jesus did this for us. He took the pain of our sins and mistakes so that we wouldn't have to be punished."

That's grace. My son remembers it to this day. And, through tears, so do I.

Apply this lesson to the business world when there comes a time when you must terminate someone's employment. When you fire someone, I believe you should do your best to leave the person better off than when he or she came to work for you. That is grace. As people leave your company, affirm whatever positive traits you can affirm. In my entire career, I can think of only a couple of people for whom I wouldn't be able to do that because of blatant bad behavior. I try to remain friends with the people I've had to terminate, and it's been my goal to handle each situation with grace and tenderness.

By the same token, there are times when you could fire someone with good reason, but choose not to do so. One of our employees once came to me with the admission that they had made a tax calculation error in our software with a large client.

"Okay," I said, drawing in a breath. "Which way?"

"It's not in our customer's favor," he confessed.

It was an extremely costly error, and I was within my rights to let the person go. But you know what? I didn't do it, and that person never repeated that error again.

Nor did anyone else in our company! It was a learning experience that cost us real money, so why throw that away?

HOLD ON LOOSELY

When I created the original blueprint of Genesis, I put myself as the focal point. I did that on purpose with one goal in mind. Do you remember the Norton Anti-Virus ads with the sleeves-rolled-up founder, Peter Norton, placed squarely on the front of the box? That's exactly how I created Genesis. I wanted people to understand that there was a real person behind our products—me! It was my reputation I was putting on the line to back up what every Genesis customer could expect to receive from us, in terms of quality and customer service.

If you want your company to live past you, at some point in its lifespan, you have to flip the narrative. Today it's definitively Genesis, and I happen to be here. I'll tell you about where that strategy ultimately led me in a later chapter. But there was a time in the early 2000s when, out of necessity, Genesis became less about me and more about the company as a whole after having been a one-man band for so long. I was still the one standing behind every product we made, but it was definitely no longer the Phil Burks show. It became the Genesis show, and rightfully so.

What is the downside to a decision like that? When I worked alone, I was responsible for my failures. When I hired staff to work with me, I owned their mistakes also. Someone else's errors became my responsibility—my mess to clean up, if you will. Avoid ordering The Looky Loo when someone messes up. Don't call needless attention to a mistake and embarrass someone. Deal with it, but do so in an appropriate way. You have to tolerate someone else's learning curve if you're going to expand your reach. This strategy will prove to be good for business, but it will drive a controlling personality up the wall to realize they can't control everything that happens.

Case in point. Some of our "graduates" have joined other companies, taking what they learned at Genesis and applying it in new environments. That makes me smile. I hate to lose them, but as I say, you don't raise your kids to stay with you the rest of their lives. The best and highest purpose is for them to go out and replicate and multiply whatever you invested in them.

I hired James right out of college on the recommendation of Michael, who had been working for us for about five years at that point. Working on a startup project within a small company like ours, the developers did it all. They wrote the code, tested it, wrote the documentation, answered support calls, attended trade shows, performed on-site installations, and led training sessions. Once I assigned a task, I trusted my employees to do it even better than I would do it. James was attending college at the time I hired him, and Genesis offered him our college tuition reimbursement program:

100% reimbursement for an A, 80% for a B, 0% for a C. You had to pay Genesis if you failed a course!

After three years, by his own admission, James relied on some bad advice he received in college about needing to change jobs every few years just to stay "relevant and hirable." So, he went to work at software Company X on the other side of town for almost double what we could afford to pay. They were expanding their development team and looking to hire developers with experience.

I was disappointed to lose James, but happy for him to follow his instincts and to make a higher wage. The culture shock he experienced at his new job was a revelation, to say the least. He later compared it to trying to build a spaceship out of bone knives and bearskins (a reference for all of you Star Trek fans). Culture is very important to Genesis, and he missed the level of innovation and excitement that was absent at Company X. More than once, James said, the owner called all employees together to tell them they were useless and he was shutting down the company. Thirteen months into his new job, James wrote me an email that simply said: "Daddy, can I come home?"

How could I resist? When we met for lunch to discuss coming back, James told me something so wise, and I often use it when I speak to audiences.

"Phil," he said, "I learned at Company X why the grass is greener on the other side of the fence. It's because of the way the cow is facing! I got pooped on almost daily!"

I hate to put words in his mouth, especially when he writes this:

"Over the years, Genesis has evolved to be a much larger company. Yet, somehow, as the company has grown, so has the company's compassion for its employees and community. As a person, I have grown with the company. When I started at Genesis, I was a single, cigarette-smoking, Red Bull-chugging code monkey and borderline video game addict. Today, I am a married father of two girls, non-smoking, tea-chugging, SCRUM-certified Product Owner with 20 years of professional software development (who occasionally plays video games). I serve as past President of the Whitehouse ISD Education Foundation and am Mayor of the City of Whitehouse. My professional and personal development was possible because Genesis provided me with a strong career foundation and invested in me. I am honored to be a part of the Genesis family, and I am proud of what we do for our employees, our community, and the markets that we serve around the world."

WHICH WAY IS UP?

How do you hold something or someone you care about loosely? The same way parents do with their children.

When my kids were little, I was their protector. I watched out for them because that was my number one job. But as they become adults, the curve flattens out a bit, and the role changes over time. The hands-on approach you used when your kids were young is too stifling for an adult child in their late twenties. By that time, they are responsible for molding themselves based on the principles you taught them early on.

I was not a helicopter parent. I was a get-out-of-the-way parent because I wanted my kids to be responsible for who they became. And I am so proud to say that they have become exactly who I hoped they'd be. Many times, in spite of me! I used the same method at Genesis. My goal was always to get out of the way so the people could grow and become who they needed to be—and that included helping them learn from their mistakes.

I wasn't successful overnight—although I wanted to be! Like anyone else just starting out, I wanted instant everything. Then when I was older, I made the mistake of praying for patience instead. You better be careful with that. Why? Because you're going to get what you asked for. And you'll learn the tough lessons. God sometimes put me through difficult experiences where I could not understand which way was up. Was he directing my life in any discernable way, or was I actually on my own? At the next stage of my life, I wasn't always sure.

EIGHT

The Regret on Rye

In the early days of Genesis around 2000, I didn't have enough money coming in to cover our expenses. There were periods when I could not cover payroll for two or even three months. We were trying to negotiate a huge new contract that would result in hundreds of thousands of dollars in profit for the company—but it was taking much longer and consuming many more reams of paper to land the plane.

I was transparent with my employees about our cash flow and asked them to "hang in there with me" until I could pay them. I knew that the future of Genesis was clearly spectacular, based on all the existing and new business we were developing. But the present moment was a true test of faith. I wrote an email to employees that said, in part:

This may be a rocky ride for a while. When MANY companies are laying off employees, WE are NOT. Each one of you has a job if you can hang with us. Each of you is 100% important to all of this happening. It will not happen if you give less than 100%. I'm in here with most of you that live paycheck to paycheck. I look at the numbers, just like you, and I have to decide just like you, "Do I have a paycheck coming? Do I have a future? What do I tell my landlord?" My answer to myself is yes. Hang with me. I hope your conclusion is the same, and you'll continue to believe in where we all are headed.

During that same challenging period, the IRS bills kept coming, and I made a definitive choice.

THE CHOICE THAT HAUNTS ME

I chose to pay my employees with what little money I had coming in, rather than paying the IRS. For the next two years, I received increasingly stern notices and scary phone calls regarding my mounting IRS debt.

"Well, we can work this out, Mr. Burks," the voice on the other line would tell me, advising me to make sure I at least kept up with the penalty and interest.

The problem at that point was that the penalty and interest alone were much more than the original tax bill itself! It was egregious.

Things took a very dark turn for the worse when I took a flight to Jakarta, Indonesia, to do some work for Motorola to install and train the software I had written. I had negotiated the invoice for $10,000, which was more than we had seen in months. I landed bleary-eyed after a very long flight over the Pacific and listened to my voicemail on my way to baggage claim. There was an unusual message from my CPA telling me to call Bobbie immediately, no matter the time.

That was strange, I thought. Why would my CPA leave me a message about calling my wife?

What happened next remains the single most deeply painful event in my life. I called Bobbie. That morning, she had gone to the radio station where she worked to pick up her paycheck. A man in a black suit was waiting for her.

"Thank you. I'll take that," he'd said and whisked the envelope containing her paycheck right out of her hands.

"What in the world is going on, Phil?" Bobbie rightfully wanted to know. Her tone was serious and frightened.

I had no idea the IRS would garner Bobbie's wages to pay for MY business tax debt. I had never told her what was happening with the IRS because, in my arrogance, I thought I would figure out a way to fix it. She would not have to be bothered with it. My motive may have been good, but it was totally wrong of me to attempt fixing this on my own.

When I heard the pain in her voice, I was 10,000 miles away. In that moment, I could do absolutely nothing to help her and make it right. I leaned heavily against the wall of the hallway where I was standing in the Jakarta terminal and slid all the way down to the floor, holding my cellphone to my ear with trembling fingers as throngs of people walked around me.

I felt tears stinging my eyes and asked myself, "What have I done? How stupid can I be?"

It was one of the darkest moments I've ever experienced. Thinking I could handle this situation on my own, I realized I had lied to my bride by not involving her in the IRS storm that was brewing. Regret doesn't even begin to describe the enormity of my personal disappointment. I sat for what seemed like 30 minutes, praying and asking for forgiveness. Asking for help. I was going over every possible solution to this problem while I was on the other side of the globe.

The Regret on Rye is always served cold. It's the one Failure Sandwich that is completely avoidable. It ought to stay off the menu, but bad behavior and poor choices make it a popular item unfortunately. This chapter about The Regret on Rye is about decisions. The regret comes after the fact and after you've made the choice.

I desperately wanted to immediately fly home after I talked to Bobbie, but I had to stay in Jakarta and finish the project for our client so that I would have money to pay my employees and some of the IRS bill and, honestly, have enough to put some food on our family's table. I was now facing an IRS bill with penalty and interest that had grown to over four times the original amount of the tax bill. The stress I experienced, coupled with the embarrassment and stress I put on my wife, was almost more than I could stand.

I couldn't even begin to imagine the fear and anguish Bobbie was experiencing. I begged God to help me find my way through it. Meanwhile, I was stuck in Jakarta having to be a good instructor of our software to 15 students.

Thanks to a team of CPAs and friends, I ended up choosing an "offer in compromise" with the IRS, which is a complicated procedure where I paid the original bill and they forgave the penalties and interest. It's a one-time exception with the government, and I had to stay squeaky clean the next seven years—which I was more than willing and able to do.

Remember the IDATel loss from an earlier chapter? That financial loss ended up helping set the stage for the IRS offer in compromise and made it a reality. Another example of something good coming from a bad loss. For an offer in compromise, the IRS makes taxpayers do a detailed reporting of income, expenses, and potential income to determine the amount you have to pay and how you pay it. And that's IF they will allow you to participate in this program!

The large IDATel losses and Genesis' debt at that particular time, coupled with other family expenses, adjusted our income very low and showed that we were good candidates. This time, I shared this process, painful as it was, with my bride. No more surprises on the IRS front. I borrowed money from friends, from life insurance, and scraped together cash to make the one-time payment that was roughly equivalent to the root amount owed to the IRS, minus all penalties and interest.

I still have all the paperwork from this episode, including the letter from the IRS showing that I had successfully completed the program and was in good standing. I was eventually able to pay back my friends (with interest) and put the life insurance money back in place.

If I think I did the right thing by paying my employees instead of the IRS, I must balance it with the shame and agony that came with the failure. Yes, I broke the law of the land. Yes, I put my wife through horrible, needless pain by hiding this problem from her. In that sense, I technically should have let Genesis die, paid off my tax bill, and called it a day.

But for the two employees who are still with me today after making it through that time, it's a different story. They are leaders with thriving careers and real estate and wonderful families. They are on the cutting edge of our work at Genesis that is transforming our industry and helping save lives. Was it right for me to skip my tax payment and pay my employees instead? Ethically, was it right? I still don't know the answer all these years later. Sometimes the outcome of our biggest failures and regrets is TBD—To Be Determined.

MONEY COMES AND GOES

The context of this story is about money, plain and simple. Money, when not handled right, can lead to all kinds of regret. When I was young, my parents modeled the proper place of money. I received a dollar allowance each week in coins. My mom set up three empty jars on our kitchen counter—a mayonnaise jar, a mustard jar, and a pickle jar. My parents taught me to put 10% of my dollar to give to God and 10% in savings, while the other 80% went into the pickle jar to do what I wanted with it.

I was an avid model builder, so most of that money went to buy the latest model car. Try to figure out how to do this 10/10/80 plan, if you aren't doing so already. It's hard. I haven't always done it when I was younger in business—and not because of a lack of desire but because I was barely surviving.

As crazy as it may sound, money is the least of your concerns. Don't pray and hope for money in business. Pray and hope instead for wisdom—that some of life's greatest lessons are taking root inside of you as you try and do the right things. Once you get wisdom, everything else in life is bug spit in comparison. The money will come and go.

Had I been praying for wisdom during the IRS-gate, I know the outcome would have been very different. In business, if you try to get money without acquiring wisdom, you may have a fat bank account but not necessarily for long because you won't make wise choices. The goal is that you're learning to act more carefully and purposefully, and then all the right things, including money, will fall into place around that. If you're curious, read Matthew 6:33 for an idea of what I'm talking about.

BE STRAIGHTFORWARD, NOTHING LESS

Another indelible lesson I learned from being served The Regret on Rye is the principle of being straightforward with the stakeholders in every situation. In this IRS example, my employees were some of the stakeholders. But the biggest stakeholder was my wife, my life partner, and I neglected her. I wanted to keep this problem quiet until I could address it, but I was not able to fix it!

Because the situation happened early on in my business, it primed me to become what some people call "full kimono." Being full kimono means you tell others the truth, good or bad, and this positions you to openly receive feedback and information that may influence the choices you make. This full kimono principle is also what undergirds the purpose of having family meetings—to let all the members of the family hear the information that potentially affects them and to give them a chance to voice their views. In this way, all the interested parties have bought into what happens next. They are part of the success—or failure—of the key decisions you make.

I've learned how to tell the bad news in a business setting and then ask for help from employees and others. Trust me, this approach works very well. Admit your weaknesses, and let those who mean the most to you come alongside and help because, believe it or not, they WANT to help.

I want our employees to know what's being thought about and talked about in our business. The decisions and direction we take as a company are ultimately the responsibility of those charged with leadership, but there is a proverb about "many minds producing knowledge." This word of wisdom is from King Solomon, one of the most famous kings in Jewish history. If a king needed the counsel of many, you and I might also do well to seek it.

DON'T DO BUSINESS ALONE

If you don't want to experience the agony of having to eat The Regret on Rye, there is something else you can do. Don't do business alone. Don't do business relying on yourself and maybe one other person. You need a cord of three strands, the third leg of the stool, that third voice to keep you from making decisions in a vacuum. Employees can provide that third perspective the senior leadership alone cannot provide. And in my case, in addition to myself and my employees, prayer is a huge, stable leg of that stool.

It's like Facebook—if all your friends are the ones who always like your posts, you get the false notion that you're right about virtually everything! If you are a leader, put yourself in a court of law, figuratively speaking, when you're facing a tough decision. Listen to all sides of an argument to deepen your understanding of your options. That's how you can fine-tune the alternatives. The worst thing you can do is to make rash judgments when what's needed is informed decisions.

My dad was the wisest man I ever knew. When he was working at home in the garage on his projects, he would measure in his head several times before he would take the next step. I likewise enjoy pondering my options, and it's well-known that I research something to the infinite degree whenever I am deciding on the best course of action, from making a major purchase for the house to something having to do with business. You don't want to know the amount of copious research that went into my first Can-Am Spyder purchase. Seriously, no.

I find myself going back to the ol' list of pros and cons, but I make sure I'm arriving at the wisest point of action, not just identifying the path of least resistance. Think about a decision you need to make. What is the easiest path, and what is the wisest and best path?

Typically, I approach decisions with 90% logic and reserve only about 10% for emotion. I'll take half an hour to step back from a hard call I need to make and think it through. Hopefully, that's a lesson I'll continue to carry with me—God knows I've been working on it since my twenties.

PACE YOURSELF

Another way to combat eating too many of The Regret on Rye sandwiches is to limit SAYING what you may regret, especially in personal and business conversations. A quiet man stands in contrast to a fool, I've since learned. But have you noticed how much people love to be right? They love to be the first to speak up and then say later, "I told you so."

I used to have that same drive. It's natural to want to feel significant, you know. But I hold my tongue and leave the prognostication to the experts these days. I'm satisfied just to know that God's got this, whatever happens. And I have too much behind me, including many potholes and several twists and turns, to let this world worry me now. I have to moderate my comments at this point. It's not that I *don't* worry—I still do. But I realize it doesn't do any good except churn up my stomach. My worries come in much shorter bursts these days.

In other words, as you age, you learn to pace yourself when offering an opinion. That strategy generally leads to having fewer regrets. It's vital to get as much information as you can before jumping to conclusions and making the call on a decision. I've learned to modify my life over time to take whatever happens in stride. If there's a loud bang in a room, I'm not the guy who leaps to his feet in alarm. I'm going to assess the situation first. I've also learned not to be the first or loudest voice speaking in the room. I'd rather be the last and quietest voice in the room. Because that means I was listening and learning. See what I mean? Less regret.

Fred Smith is the epitome of listening intently with both ears to what someone has to say. He asks some softball follow-up questions, but he also asks his fair share of the hard questions. "What do you mean by that? What causes you to think that way?" I often find that my meetings with Fred are a reminder that I can listen and evaluate far better than I can talk on the fly!

I've also learned from Fred and others to answer questions completely. You know, the opposite of what politicians do! You won't regret what you say to others if you give people useful answers that hopefully have meaning.

There's a story of a man flying in a helicopter in Washington State when the fog rolled in, blocking visibility. He climbed above the dense fog, but he became disoriented. Finally, he saw a high-rise building poking its head above the mist. He flew close enough to make eye contact with the workers inside the glass walls of the building. He scribbled on a piece of paper, "WHERE AM I?" and held it up to the windshield. The workers quickly scratched a sign that read, "YOU'RE IN A HELICOPTER." The pilot thanked them and navigated to a safe landing back at the airport. He related the story to his friends later who were curious how that answer helped him navigate to safety. He replied, "Simple. I knew I was at the headquarters of a major global IT firm. Who else could give me an answer that was technically accurate yet totally useless?" Get the message?

Maybe that's part personality; maybe it comes with age. I know that my mentor Bernie's first reaction to anything that happens is not to offer his opinion. Instead, he says, "Let's pray about that."

That kind of habit does two things that work in your favor. Number one, it's prayer. Studies have shown that it has benefits even for the non-religious. And two, prayer has a way of slowing you down and letting you think through the options. Prayer is an automatic pause that releases some pressure so that you can process what's happening and make the best choices that come with fewer disappointments and heartaches. Talk about lowering your regret score!

When I pray, I try to talk 20% of the time and listen hard 80%. How does somebody listen to God? Do you sit there and twiddle your thumbs? Or do you listen by digging into Scripture to see what God shows you? I think that's one of the primary ways God speaks. Sometimes I've looked at passages in the Bible 15 million times in the past and suddenly a new insight jumps out at me.

When people ask for my opinion, I've learned to respond, "I don't have enough information to form an opinion yet," if more information is needed. Those truthful little words have saved me from making an uninformed statement I'll regret later, and it's saved many a friendship. But it takes restraint to hold back and do your research before you speak.

In my twenties through fifties, my way of following this principle was very poorly executed. I would just "hole up" and not say anything. I would have tons of thoughts swirling in my head, but nothing would come out of my mouth for fear it would be so vitriolic and hurtful. Sometimes I wanted to let it fly, but I just could not get my brain and mouth to connect while under the stress of the situation.

That approach backfired hundreds of times, yet I didn't learn how to handle things better until I was in my late fifties. Am I perfect at responding to others? Heavens, no. But I can now frame the words, "I need some time to (process, pray, research, etc.)..." far more often than I used to.

To this day, I am still afraid of what might come out of my mouth, which is why in my twenties and thirties I read a chapter a day in Proverbs, one of the Wisdom Books of the Old Testament. It's my favorite book in the Bible to this day. If you read one chapter a day for a month, you'll have 31 readings in a month. I have read through Proverbs over and over to get wisdom because I realize that what the Bible says is true: you have everything if you have wisdom. It will help you view life in the proper perspective—and see that what you consider bad is really something for your good in disguise. Sometimes when you are tearfully chowing down on The Regret on Rye, you realize that time really does heal all wounds. And you see something good coming out of a situation.

A GOLDEN OPPORTUNITY

Here's an example. I can safely say that the building Genesis occupies today was because of a thing called "rebanding"—something that was initially a total pain in our industry. Rebanding is like changing the tires on a fully-loaded bus that's rolling down the highway at 65mph. You cannot stop; you must figure out how to do it on the go. And it's not fun.

When Nextel built out their nationwide push-to-talk radio system, it was discovered that some frequencies on which they were operating interfered with public safety two-way radios. I saw this interference firsthand while working on a new product we were co-developing with Dictaphone. One day we were at the master site for all of Harris County, Texas, and every-so-often some of our radios would simply stop working. I walked outside to get some air and noodle on the problem when I saw what I thought was a cellular tower in their parking lot. I came back in and made a call to a Nextel friend on the inside. Sure enough, I learned that it was one of their sites. When certain transmitters of theirs would come on, our radios stopped working!

After a long set of hearings on the matter, the FCC ruled that the government would reband the frequencies and thus move public safety to other sets of frequencies. They also ruled that Nextel would pay for the huge amount of work to reband. Since the majority of the public safety two-way radio systems in existence are manufactured by Motorola, they were tapped with performing most of the work. In turn, Motorola then turned to Genesis to help with some of their more stubborn software that would not change over to the new frequencies.

It was a pain for the FCC to have to do it. It was a pain for Nextel to have to pay for it. And it was a pain for Motorola and Genesis to accomplish it. But, man, did it pay off for our little company!

First, Genesis could add significant infrastructure and more employees immediately to do the work. Second, Motorola licensed us for more of their proprietary technology, and we got to work enhancing our existing software to work with these newly rebanded radio systems. That handful of software products for rebanding launched us into the next level of Genesis. Third, we now had enough cash in the bank to build a bigger building to hold all our increased capacity. It should have been relatively easy to make the move, but the story of how we moved to our new building is a doozy.

DREAMING A LITTLE DREAM

With the influx of income and staff, I started thinking

about building a new permanent location for Genesis because we were still renting office space in a large building with other tenants. There's a tipping point where if you're renting a building, you're not building the company's assets. You're just maintaining an expense. If you can figure out how to do it, it's usually not a bad idea to build a brick and mortar location you can be proud of. It takes a long time to pay it off, but you are building equity.

I never went upstairs to the second floor of our rented office building except to go to the restroom or to see my friend and mentor, Fred Smith, who also had an office there. One day I went upstairs and got in a caffeine-infused conversation with some engineering fellows who also worked in that building. We found out that both of our companies were looking to construct office buildings because we were tired of renting. There are no coincidences, you remember. That coffee and conversation eventually led all the way to the building that houses Genesis today.

In further discussions with the engineering firm, we decided I would build the new building, and they would lease back the space from Genesis. I was more than ready by this time to move out of the rental office space. About the only thing I would really miss was having great feet-up-on-the-desk conversations most Friday mornings with Fred.

The land where I wanted to build Genesis' new office

was across town and cost about one million dollars. As I considered this staggering amount, I thought to myself, "How am I EVER going to get a loan to do this?"

I'd never even thought about that kind of number! When the appraisal came through at slightly more than the sale price, I took it as a sign to move forward. If things went south, I could at least sell the land for what it was worth and get out from under the note.

I then began meeting with the architect at the same engineering firm that would lease from us. I told him off the top that I did not want to build something average. I'm just not that way. Buildings tell a story, and I wanted this one to speak volumes about what could be done in East Texas in commercial real estate.

To start, I wanted lots of glass, three stories, and a glass elevator to a rooftop garden. Then we began researching the United States Green Building Council (USGBC) to understand their LEED certification standards. Basically, we learned, you accrue points if your design has certain elements like energy-efficient glass, air conditioning, lighting, etc. You can also get points for incorporating a mass transit bus stop near your building. With an eye on earning the LEED Silver certification, we designed a geothermal heating and air conditioning system that would draw water from 100 wells, all 300 feet deep, to help cool the building. The plans even called for a data center in the hillside to take advantage of the cool earth.

I was very vocal in our community in my enthusiasm for the new Genesis building. Local television stations interviewed me about the innovative design, and I spoke at Chamber events about the unique components built into our plans. I even wrote a blog about it! In every setting, I was very clear that God was in and through this venture and emphasized that I knew he was leading me down this path for his glory.

ENTER: PROBLEM, STAGE RIGHT

When I priced out the 30,000 square foot structure, it came to about $320 per square foot. This was in 2009 where $160 per square foot would get you a nice house! The plan called for the tenant to lease half the space, and Genesis would occupy the other half. It was about 10 million dollars in construction costs—a crazy high figure. Worse yet, the appraisal of the building would not shake out, no matter what magic science formula the experts applied. It still came up about $1.5 million short.

I was undeterred. I knew it was God's plan, so it was going to work out, right? I continued to be very outspoken in our community about how Genesis was building a model for commercial real estate in East Texas and beyond. I was sincere and determined to do this and spent hours with a calculator and a notepad trying to crunch and re-crunch the numbers.

Then I started down the Small Business Association (SBA) route and finally got together a workable formula that included my cash, an SBA loan, and other liens against the property itself. I was all-in, no question, and it was scary. But I was confident that I was doing the right thing because I had prayed and prayed about it. I had even asked God to throw up roadblocks if I was not supposed to do it.

The day finally came when my banker met with his CEO to sign off on my loan. The banker would later replay the scene for me. The CEO had the pen in his hand, about to sign, when he put the pen down and said he would prefer to see a signed lease from the tenant before he approved the loan.

When I heard this news, I told my banker that would be no problem, even though I was already thinking of the serious delays this would cause. I had also paid $900,000 out of my own pocket for some initial progress on a parking lot, rainwater capture system, irrigation, and other infrastructure, so time was of the essence to secure the capital.

There was something else at play behind the scenes that I did not know at the time. As promised, I contacted the tenant for a signed lease agreement, and they went radio silent. I soon learned they had been bought out by a much larger national corporation that was not interested in leasing from Genesis. Needless to say, I did not get the loan.

The dream was exploding in front of my eyes. I was beyond discouraged. I was very embarrassed that I had been so public about this being a great witness for God, and now the whole thing was cratering around me. I experienced the Kübler-Ross model of the Stages of Grief over the deal. (Did I mention I'm married to a licensed professional counselor?) I was in denial. Then I was angry. I even tried bargaining with God and almost fell into a depression about it before I could finally accept what had happened.

I sat down to tackle The Regret on Rye. By now, I regretted saying anything publicly about building a new building. I regretted spending the money. I regretted ever thinking that I could take on such a challenge and succeed. I took bite after bite of The Regret on Rye, but then something started to change mid-chew.

THAT'S THE TICKET!

I turned to another local architect and friend, Steve Fitzpatrick, who probably felt as if he spent the first two sessions counseling me! But he said something very wise in our initial meeting.

"You know, Phil," he offered. "I don't think your dream is dead. I think it's just changed." That's what you do with The Regret on Rye. If you made a bad decision, pivot. Learn all you can from it and then change—take a new step. Everyone has regrets, but you have to keep going.

In my case, Steve advised me to consider a new design that stripped out the unnecessary expensive items just to achieve a LEED certification and used replacements that were still uber-cool and exceptionally energy-efficient without breaking the bank.

Chasing the points for Silver LEED certification wasn't worth it in the end. Sure, I could build a bus stop that would earn 8 points, but it would require an ADA compliant walkway that cost about $280,000 in concrete. We could earn 5 points for a bicycle rack, but even that little detail was $1000 and would kick off a chain of fiscally irresponsible moves. Employees biking to work meant building showers in the 90-degree summers in Texas where we live. And showers meant men's and women's locker rooms. You see where this is going. At some point there must be an ROI (Return On Investment) for all of the energy-saving design measures you put in a building.

Steve's brilliant plan took advantage of a flat place on the same 30-acre tract we had purchased, instead of burrowing into the hillside with budget-busting retaining walls from my original plan. My geothermal HVAC system was costing one million dollars alone in the initial plan, not to mention the fact that the steel to withstand the weight of a garden rooftop was also tremendously pricey.

He also encouraged me to research other office designs that spoke to me. I am fortunate to have traveled the world enough to see how different cultures design their offices. In Japan, for example, office design translates to desks in straight rows like elementary school, with the manager of a department on a platform at the end of each row. That says something about their work culture. What did I want to say about ours?

Using the design talents of Steve and Brian at Fitzpatrick and Associates, what Genesis ended up with is 17,500 square feet of amazing office space. When I saw them pouring the foundation, it was a very gratifying sight. I walked the property scores of times, praying for God to give wisdom and to bless what we were doing.

I talk freely about failure and regret at this point in my story because I want people to know that failure lays the foundation. Foundation work is the ugly and mostly unseen (but necessary) part of constructing beautiful buildings—and life is no different. Some of the most beautiful and successful endeavors are built on failure because someone decided they would keep going forward and not quit when times got tough. At our grand opening, we held a ribbon cutting ceremony with a braided strand of CAT 5 network cables and released two doves in a nod to our Genesis logo. It was a sweet day, and God got the glory.

REGRET LEADS TO SOMEWHERE UNEXPECTED

I began this story to convince you that something good can come from something bad. Regret can lead to a beautiful place. In our case, I like to say that our building today is not "green" but light tan! Our HVAC is not geothermal, but our Daikin air conditioner has an immeasurable SEER rating, according to the experts who measure that kind of thing. We capture rainwater, store it in a 36,000-gallon cistern, and pump it up to irrigate the beautiful landscaping. We have high-efficiency glass and even installed a white roof for additional energy savings. The proof in the pudding for me was going outside one day in the middle of two weeks of 100-plus temperatures to see that our 200kw natural gas generator was pulling just 74kw! Phenomenal. Our electricity bill is not zero, but it's half of what you'd expect for an average building of this size.

Buildings do tell stories, and they capture the core values of companies. When we were looking at various office designs, I looked at a nearby building that was for sale. I walked the narrow halls and saw that every office had floor-to-ceiling walls and a closed door. Like a closet. It had such a dead feel. No collaboration. No community. Everyone was isolated. At that moment, I swore I would never build a building that looked like that. We designed a few segregated offices in our new building, but most of Genesis is open space. I did not go the full-on cubicle route. When you peer over a horizon of cubicles, it has a cold look to me. Instead, we incorporated pods that give more of a collaborative feel.

I like to see the people I'm working with, so we also used glass interior walls. Yes, it added to the expense. But our employees can see the trees and birds outside while they work. They stay appraised of the weather and get a sense of being part of a high-tech campus tucked into the woods.

People who walk into Genesis immediately get a sense of confidence and creativity; they understand the details were not done as an afterthought. We "programmed it" with architectural language that promotes collaboration, creativity, and innovative designs. Visitors quickly understand that we are real and here to stay. CHIFF is an acronym we use to describe our core values at Genesis, and it stands for Clever, High Quality, Innovative, Functional, and Fun. It's a baseline standard for everything we do here, from advertising, to software, to the way we treat customers. This building is CHIFF.

We are humbled by the awards the building has won. We stand out because we're different—especially for East Texas. We have had the pleasure of hosting people from all over the world for tours. The highest compliment I have received to date was from a commercial developer from the Bay Area who took a tour with a mutual friend and exclaimed, "This building looks like it belongs in Northern California!" That's not something that happens every day around these parts.

THE VALUE OF BEING PREPARED TO CHANGE

As I'm writing this book, the idea of "work space" is on many people's minds because the majority of the world's workforce sheltered in place during the pandemic. And many are not returning to the office anytime soon. During the early days of COVID-19, most of our employees gathered up their monitors and worked from home. We, like the rest of the world, missed the watercooler conversations about family and kids, but work carried on.

I don't believe the COVID-19 pandemic is the last one to happen. There will be others. Tougher times are ahead. We were lulled to sleep, and this has been a wake-up call to be better prepared regarding the way we design and operate our work-related infrastructure. What if the Internet went down nationwide or worldwide in the future? What if a sunspot knocks out our power grid? That's not "the sky is falling" rhetoric or science fiction anymore. It's real. How well are businesses set up to pivot during those potential scenarios?

Something like a sunspot is 100% out of our control, as is the associated Electro Magnetic Pulse (EMP) that could render much of the technological infrastructure of the United States useless in the 20 minutes it takes for an EMP to travel to Earth. An EMP pulse from a lightning bolt is a high-voltage charge that has a role in creating the "pow!" of energy you see and hear during a storm. When scientists tested the atomic bomb, they learned there is a huge EMP associated with it that is just as dangerous and destructive as the massive heat resulting from the explosion.

Thankfully, our ionosphere helps guard the Earth against EMPs. But if the solar flare was big enough and strong enough to make it past our protective shield, we would have only minutes to prepare before the EMP would take out everything from electronic equipment to power substations. At Genesis, we incorporated a giant generator that could keep us online if the power grid goes down. It's powered by natural gas here in Texas, because if natural gas ever goes away, well then, we might as well just all go home! The data feed to the outside world is fiber optic, which also helps keep us alive!

What will happen in the future? I don't know. I'm a bad prognosticator. I never wanted to be good at that kind of thing because if you're right, you're an expert. If you're wrong, you're just stupid. I try to choose the wisdom route, which often means keeping your mouth shut and letting the future be what it will be. But one thing COVID-19 has taught us all is the value of being prepared. That alone can lead to less regrets.

GETTING GOOD AT MESSING UP

Over time I have learned that my God is a God of opposites. Usually what I'm thinking should be done in a situation is the reverse of how it plays out. I can see that in the story of how our Genesis building went from one design to another to get us to the exact space we were supposed to occupy. But why did God let me experience so much regret at first? Why let me be so vocal about the original building that didn't make? I tried so hard, but we just couldn't get it to go, and it failed. It bugs me to this day. Why couldn't I have started with the plans for this building we're in now and saved the public embarrassment?

My main beef about what happened is that I am a man of my word. My word is my bond, just like God's Word is his bond. If I say I'm going to do something, I do it. Even if it hurts me or costs me money, I want to stay by my word. If I promise someone something, I follow through. (This is proving problematic for me the older I get because a lot of times I forget what I said! If I have ever not followed through, it's not due to malice. I simply forgot, so go easy, okay?)

Of course, no one in my circle of friends, family, or colleagues thought that I'd failed. They were blown away by the new building we ended up with, and the original plans faded way into a storage closet. But this experience remains a question mark and conundrum for me about why I had to fail before I succeeded.

The good news in all this is that the more you fail, the better at it you become. The more Regret on Rye sandwiches you eat, the more you realize that even though you may have some regrets, you can put it all back together. You're battered, but you're breathing. You're still here. It's why people practice anything—to get better at it. Athletes run the same drills on the field over and over. Pilots run the same checklists before they fly. Business is the same way. You get better at failure the more you do it. Believe me, the third or fourth time the "worst thing that can happen" happens, it ain't so bad.

As our new building was being constructed, I'd admittedly focused 90% of my attention on it. I do NOT regret having invested my daily attention to the building's details. However, I left the team that represented the best Genesis had to offer without their leader's full attention during that time. I had hoped that the momentum of a "team concept" would work better than it did, and I realized I had to take responsibility for the fact that it didn't work as well as I had hoped.

Due to my lack of leadership, we did not get where I wanted us to be as an organization at the time the building opened. The domino effect that followed was as much of a surprise to me as anyone, as I'll explain next.

NINE

The Double Decker Doozy

was weighing an important decision in the spring of 2013, which happened to be the year of my 61st birthday and the average age when people start early retirement. For many years, I had moaned to my wife (and anyone who would listen) about how much I wanted to have a motorcycle. Bobbie patiently listened to me, but common sense overruled. We were busy raising kids at the time and knew it was best not to add a potential problem into our lives. But there eventually came a point when it felt as if it might be the right timing when we had less family responsibilities and more free time. In fact,

for Christmas one year, Bobbie gave me a gift certificate
for a Motorcycle Safety Training Course. The card read,
"Time to put up or shut up, old man!" That's my wife.

I took the course, passed the Department of Public
Safety driving test, and then went shopping one Saturday
morning after weeks of online research. I came home
that afternoon with a lightly used black 2010 Can Am
Spyder RT that we soon christened "Darth." Bobbie and
I purchased helmets, and off we went together on the
blacktop country roads of East Texas. Bobbie quickly
learned that the view sitting behind her 6'1" husband is
not stellar, so she promptly got her motorcycle license
and her own Spyder we named "Psycho," since she is a
psychotherapist.

Without a doubt, "ryding" Spyder motorcycles has
reinvigorated our empty nest season of life, which is
another area of big change for most people of a certain
age. I call the motorcycles one of our bottles of "empty
nest glue" that keeps it all together! We're on different
motorcycles, but we talk on the helmet comms the entire
way. We laugh, we read silly signs out loud, we grimace
at the strange smells you don't catch in a car, and we
make memories with friends in the Spyder community.

Let me ask you something. What will be your empty
nest glue when you get to that time in your life, the
time when your children leave? The point when you
are considering retiring? My advice to you is the same
advice that someone else gave to me. Don't wait to begin

enjoying life and the fruit of your labor. If you don't have your health later, you'll regret so much what you never did with the people you love.

In the past, those who retired from a lifetime of service from a single company received the "gold watch" at the going away party and that was that. They twiddled their thumbs and played golf until they finally died. Lots of things change when you hit your sixties, and you start rethinking your priorities and what you're going to do with the time you have left on the clock.

We had been in our beautiful new building just a short while when something unexpected happened. I truly didn't see it coming until the moment I was looking straight at it, but in the span of one weekend everything would change for me and also for Genesis.

WHO SAID ANYTHING ABOUT RETIREMENT?

With the building construction behind us, I was looking for my next "big thing" when Jim, one of our senior executives, initiated a Friday afternoon conversation. I opened his lengthy email and sat back in my chair, thinking about what I read. Jim had been with Genesis about four years, and he had done an excellent job in his role as vice-president for Business Development. He came to Genesis after starting and running high-tech companies in the heat of the PC growth phase in Austin, Texas. After reading his email, I asked him to meet me at the office Saturday morning when it would be nice and quiet.

There comes a point in the life of every company president when the role outgrows him or her. As I drove home Friday and pondered Jim's email, I feared he was right about two things. One, Genesis was at that point. And two, I was not nearly as talented at spinning plates as I thought I was! On Saturday morning after we talked, sadly, I knew he was right on both counts.

Changing jobs or evolving into new roles is The Double Decker Doozy because not only are you grieving the loss of what WAS, you're not sure how to deal with what IS. This Failure Sandwich requires your letting go of the past and finding your way in the future—all at the same time. Proceed cautiously and slowly as you walk through this part of life one step, one bite, and one chew at a time. It can be confusing and depressing.

When I read Jim's letter, a part of me wanted to push back and say that I could continue to do it all. How so? For starters, I'd ALWAYS done it all! I was the Founder, President, and CEO, and I'd grown accustomed to the ultimate responsibility and liability resting on my shoulders. The thought of being "the buck stops here" guy scares people who are not wired for entrepreneurship, and I get that. But it's the very thing that makes serial entrepreneurs like me get out of bed in the mornings. Entrepreneurs are the only people willing to work 90 hours a week to avoid working 40 hours for someone else. And they wouldn't have it any other way.

Worst case scenario, if everyone left Genesis, I always

knew I could count on myself in the end. And I was okay with that. Now someone else wanted my job—and he was making a strong case that he could do it better—and I was not okay with that. Not at first.

CHANGING MY MIND ABOUT CHANGING MY ROLE

It was a dark weekend. I did some heavy soul-searching about my past ability as a leader and what I should do for the company's sake in the future. That ushered in other memories and reflections on how I felt I had failed as a husband in my marriage, as a dad, and the list went on. I again heard Miss Yoder's words about being a stupid kid. My chest was tight, and I didn't sleep much. Imposter syndrome was in full force.

The Genesis Group had outgrown my abilities, and now I had to step back so it could move forward. Bobbie helped me to see this very clearly when she observed, "Phil, you love Genesis. It's your baby. What is the best thing for Genesis?"

Genesis was my baby, but no longer just my baby. I had to learn how to let go. I had to think of the business as a child whom I'd raised to go out into the world one day. When I gave my daughters away at their weddings to start new families, it was a symbol that another man was in charge now. As their dad, I had taken my daughters as far as I could, and their wedding days marked a point in time when I could no longer interfere in their daily affairs. Likewise, I had to find the courage to let Genesis move ahead of where I was so that it could be all that it was supposed to be.

I have always believed in researching "the biggest and the best" companies to glean insights that I could apply to Genesis. Two of my favorite books are *Built to Last* and *Good to Great*, both by Jim Collins. He advises a company to grow from the inside "in order to put an end to the beginning." We had a good beginning to Genesis, and now we had the opportunity to move past that in an attempt to be "great." I had made a conscious and purposeful effort to make it less about me and make it more about Genesis. But somehow in my thinking I had not taken me out of that picture entirely.

I also drew from Motorola's experience when their CEO named a new president who would handle the day-to-day operations, leaving the CEO with the self-appointed task of being Motorola's ambassador. I envisioned a similar structure where the president would report directly to me, but my primary role would be forging new partnerships and initiatives that raised the value of Genesis.

The Genesis Group had outgrown my abilities, but I had also developed other talents in the meantime. It was God's timing for me to take the chance to use them and tap into my other passions. Stepping back as president would free me up to re-prioritize my time and energy to accomplish many new things. I could expand the real estate company I'd founded, GenCore LLC., and also ramp up Corporate Green, the name of the additional land surrounding the Genesis campus that I intended to develop into office space. I could also broaden some other creative projects and partnerships that I simply had not had time to pursue. In short, I could dream again.

By Sunday morning of that life-changing weekend I knew that I needed to ask Jim a question—one that I had not considered prior to Friday.

"What if you became the president of Genesis?" I posed to him on Sunday afternoon. "And I'll be the CEO."

Jim told me his answer.

LETTING GO, ONE FINGER AT A TIME

Later that day I stared at the three-page letter to my employees that I'd just typed into Word. The words seemed to belong to someone else, but the announcement was, in fact, all mine. And so was the surprising decision the letter announced about a structural change in leadership at Genesis. It began:

> *My wife, Bobbie, and I have talked about this for about a year, and then quite a bit this past weekend. We have also prayed about it a lot. Some time ago, what needed to happen was clear. But I have struggled with making this decision...*

At the end of my letter, I assured the staff that we would all learn as we go, with everyone's help. I read the letter aloud Monday morning to everyone, and I fully admit it was a hard letter to read, filled with some tears and stops and starts to regain my composure.

I also wrote my "charge" to the new president of Genesis, highlighting eight tasks I felt would prove to be foundational to our continued success as a company. At the top of the list was the responsibility to protect the foundations of Genesis. "This is God's company, and we are stewards of the resources we have been loaned," I wrote. Following that, I talked about protecting the Genesis brand and all that it means, as well as protecting our clients that rely on our product and our people every day.

I also wanted the new president to grow all aspects of the business—not just getting new business, but also strengthening the inner workings of Genesis for the company to be built to last. In addition, I envisioned the president engaging the rest of the leadership team to do whatever it takes to work smarter, not harder, and help grow Genesis into a next-generation company that far exceeds expectations.

Of course, I listed improving profitability and protecting current income streams and working to build it out. If the new president did everything else well, the money would take care of itself. If you take care of your people and your business, it always does.

When it was time for me to hand over the reins after 24 years at the helm, I was fortunate. I had someone on board who was all-in. Jim was and is a gregarious ambassador for all things Genesis and created an infectious culture of enthusiasm that our employees loved.

The corporate culture naturally changed over time, as one would imagine it would with someone else in charge—but it did so in positive ways as the company evolved. I am the first to admit that what "drives me nuts" about the new ways we do things at Genesis is what drives the company forward. The shake-up worked out, and it worked well. Our sales more than doubled since we reached this decision. Profitability is up. Costs are down. Our president and his team are paying attention to areas I wasn't, and the growth is happening purposefully. We do more now to grow the people than I ever did, and it is showing in how our employees have taken on their own leadership roles inside and outside the company.

PERSEVERANCE IS KEY

Our condiment list is growing—the things you can do to make a Failure Sandwich more palatable. A squeeze of patience is a must. A healthy serving of prayer is on there, too. Perspective is another biggie, as I said earlier. Perseverance, used in good measure, also comes into play—especially when you are looking forward to finishing your last bite of The Double Decker Doozy and adjusting to the new role.

Make no mistake. For the first few years, it was a

difficult transition for me. Turning over the relationship with Motorola, our primary source of income at the time, was probably the most difficult move. But having watched Jim in action with Motorola over the years, I knew he would effortlessly uphold my values and the value of the Genesis brand—and he has.

Another challenge I hadn't thought too much about was finding my new role Monday-Friday. That's the Double Decker part of this Failure Sandwich—you can't go back to what was. And you're not sure what's ahead. That was tough! The hardest part involved grieving the daily process that I was no longer a part of at the office. I missed being on the firing line at Genesis, but I eventually settled for getting my mojo from a sip of coffee while looking at a Monday morning financial sheet and a dashboard of sales and cash. My heart longed—and still does to this day—for the time when I could sit down with all the individual employees and know more about them. We are a bit too big for me to do that now, but Jim and his senior leadership team make the effort to know minute details about each team member, their spouses, and children. They care for our Genesis family like their own. Jim has fostered a pastoral approach to being president of Genesis.

Me? I had to figure out what I should do next, and I had no idea what was ahead of me on that path.

Remember the scene in *The Wizard of Oz* where Toto pulls away the curtain and exposes the "Wizard" as nothing more than a mere mortal? Someday somebody's going to figure out that there are times when you don't have a clue. And hey, that's okay, too. I think one of the greatest gifts you can give to your employees and fellow team members is to assure them that the future is going to be okay no matter what happens. Leaders model the idea that we're all going to get through this together, even if somewhere inside they're thinking, "I cannot crack. I cannot crack!" Perseverance is the name of the game.

WHERE THE ROCKS ARE

It's important to pass along lessons to others in hopes they'll avoid the pitfalls that are common in business and in life. It's like the old joke about a Baptist minister, a Rabbi and a Catholic priest who go out fishing. They had been fishing all morning long when the Baptist minister realizes that he left his lunch box back at shore. He explains to his friends that he's hungry. So he stands up, steps out of the boat, walks across the water, gets his lunch out of his truck, walks back across the water, and sits down.

A few minutes later the priest says that he's been drinking his sacramental wine all morning and needs a restroom break. He steps out of the boat, walks across the water to a tree, takes care of business, walks back, and sits down next to his friends.

The Rabbi, upon seeing this, decides that if the priest and the minister can walk on water, certainly he can do so. He makes up an excuse about it being time for mid-day prayers, stands up, and starts to exit the boat. He takes one step into the water, falls in, and sinks to the bottom!

The Baptist minister turns to the Catholic priest and says, "Do you think we should have told him where the rocks are?" (Insert laugh track here.)

I use this old joke with people who need to know how life works. I've stepped out and fallen many times. But now I know where *some* of the rocks are. The rocks are below the surface—you can't see them. Just gather your courage and take the first step anyway, because a rock is there somewhere for your foot to find.

I don't understand why life works that way, or why God doesn't make the path more obvious sometimes. So I pray most mornings, "God, I have no idea where the rocks are for today, but you do. I can't see them, but I know they are there. Please put my foot where you have the rocks today." Notice—it's important to ask God to move your FOOT, not the rock. The problems you are experiencing right now can make you feel as if you're about to sink. But there are rocks out there and safe places to stand. And if you land in water up to your neck, you'll know that much more about where the rocks are next time.

Not only did I not know "where the rocks were" in this new role at Genesis, but I also discovered there were landmines everywhere! Our new president would on occasion come into my office, close the door, and let me know in no uncertain terms that I could not stick my nose back in the business.

"What?" I remember thinking the first time this scenario played out.

I didn't think I was doing that. All I did was walk through the office with a cup of coffee, I explained in my defense. Yes, I also happened to talk shop to some of the developers about a neat idea I had. No, I didn't realize that the developers had then dropped everything to tackle "the boss's idea" instead.

I knew passing the baton would be tough, but could we lighten up on the old guy? Jim was right though, dad gum it. I had always told our senior leadership, "Hire the right people, and trust them to do their job." In questioning the new president along the way, I was not following my own advice. I'd asked him to be the president, but subconsciously, I wasn't letting him do his job. Worse yet, I didn't see that I was doing that.

It took about two years for me to wrap my mind around reassigning the president's role. I think my senior team also wondered what to do with me initially. *Do we cart Phil around to trade shows? Do we just take him out back like he died?* Under Jim's leadership, everyone tried to help me make it safely around the curve.

If you are facing this Double Decker Doozy event, it can be difficult to navigate. A word of advice to those who are taking over from a founder. Help them with their transition. If it's a former mentor, boss, or even your parents as the founders of your family, there needs to be a "cold turkey" event marking the change. But after that, go to that person for advice once in a while. It helps the founder with his transition to his next phase. And even though you feel you know everything with your newly-gained power, there is still sage wisdom in the grey hairs that are on the founder's head. Tapping into that resource will pay off.

Maybe you can relate it to your parents and your kids. When your parents take on less of a daily role in the family, help them as they adjust. Do the same in business to the founder, and it will go well. One of the most satisfying opportunities you can receive as a parent is when you see your kids excel beyond your level, and in the process, they ask for your advice and help as a peer. The same applies in business transition.

These are difficult decisions to make, no matter what. What's hard about the hard decisions? We loathe change as humans. Rare is the one who likes it. Regardless of whether a longstanding pattern, habit, or role is working for us and operating at its full potential, we tend to like the fact that at least it's familiar. Too often, when life tries to move us in a different direction, it's like mating elephants—lots of snorting and grunting and waiting a long time to get results. The bigger the change, the harder it is to make it safely to the other side.

Change is difficult, said the guy who dismantled

Genesis one Friday...only to start rebuilding it anew on Monday morning. But change usually leads to the good stuff. My role today as CEO exists to guide with a passive, light hand and encourage, and that's exactly what I do at Genesis as my 70th birthday comes into focus. I probably have five more business years in me, maybe 10. I've been working a plan to gradually work less hours. I can't keep all the balls in the air like I used to do, but I'm following in my mentor Bernie's footsteps and planning all that I want to accomplish in the next decade before I hit 80.

WHAT IF A DRONE COULD SAVE LIVES?

After I changed roles at Genesis, I still had a lot on my to-do list, and I planned on taking each day as it came. But then a new project caught my eye that intrigued me immensely—and I haven't looked back since. Daniel Pink writes in his book, *DRIVE,* about what drives a person. For some, it's a financial return. For others, it's receiving recognition or awards. Pink's idea is that it's more intrinsic. One of the best motivators, he writes, is the desire to create a lasting legacy. I'm no exception, and I'm willing to bet neither are you. My foremost personal legacy is without question the relationships I've forged over the years. Second to that is the fact that Genesis software is running in many cities throughout the US and in several countries around the world helping make vital companies more efficient and even helping to save lives.

In 2014 the FCC estimated that more than 10,000

lives could be saved each year if emergency responders arrived at 911 incidents just one minute faster. I remember initially learning that fact and being compelled to do something about it.

The story of how we came up with FIRST iZ drone system begins with Genesis PULSE® in partnership with Waze®. Genesis PULSE enhances Computer-Aided-Dispatch (CADs) centers, also known as 911 Public Safety Access Points (PSAPs), so that our customers can save time, money, property, and lives by simplifying dispatch and validating their decisions as they send first responders into harm's way.

PULSE is a software tool featuring real-time live tracking and recommendations for the best ambulances and fire vehicles to respond to incidents. It also has recording and replay capabilities, along with reporting, detailed weather information, integrations with Waze, RapidSOS®, and Motorola 2-way radio locations. It allows public safety officials to see all the vehicles and personnel that need to be tracked in a single intuitive map-based display for at-a-glance confirmation that operations are as expected. Displaying active units and responses with the PULSE visual response clock makes it simple to track how fast they are responding during a crisis.

With a Google Maps-based feature that includes the satellite and traffic layers, we added the integration of a live Waze feed that displays traffic crashes, road closures, and weather alerts, so first responders see the most important information in real-time. It's all about situational awareness: knowing what they are getting into before they're there.

With the evolution of drone technology over the past few years, Genesis PULSE became much more important to public safety. FIRST iZ, the name of the drone solution, brings the entire ecosystem together and glues it with software that makes all of it work with the touch of one button.

FIRST iZ is probably one of my most passionate projects and significant achievements. It's a big deal for the industry—and it's absolutely riddled with failures, disappointments, stops, and starts—so it's the perfect last bite to serve in this book about eating a Failure Sandwich.

TEN

When Failure
Tastes Good

A notification of an accident on I-20 popped up on the Genesis PULSE screen at the ambulance provider in East Texas. The dispatcher read it and in seconds saw three more notifications of the accident, all from Waze users driving by the scene. She dispatched an ambulance on a hunch that it might be needed. ELEVEN minutes later, the official 911 call came in, just as the ambulance was already arriving on the scene! That's the kind of qualitative difference our evolving technology makes possible every day in public safety.

YOU CAN DO THAT WITH A DRONE?

Now imagine 911 dispatchers being able to deploy mission-ready drones from strategic locations like fire stations with the click of a button—many times before 911 calls are even received because of what Genesis PULSE knows about accidents. We call FIRST iZ the ultimate tool for first responders because a drone can deploy instantly and "put eyes" on the scene of a crisis almost immediately. Using live high-definition video and thermal imaging, emergency personnel can receive the information they need to respond faster, be better informed, and ultimately save more lives before they ever arrive on site.

Once launched, the drone flies to the scene up to 60mph, while simultaneously using carbon nanotubes in the belly of the bird to detect hazardous pollutants in the air to keep responders safe. This technology allows commanders to know all that they're facing beforehand. It's destined to be a fundamental player in improving emergency situations where every second counts and lives hang in the balance.

FIRST iZ is also a perfect illustration of the Failure Sandwich because of all that it's teaching me as we invent and develop it. Here's the nitty gritty stuff that this whole book is about. If you want to succeed in life, despite all the failures you may have experienced to this point, what do you have to do to make that happen? Figure that out and you'll soon discover that all the Failure Sandwiches you've been served in your lifetime will have been well worth each bite. Figure that out, and you'll agree with me that a Failure Sandwich can end up tasting pretty darn good, even though the cheese is sliding off, the tomato is falling out of the sides, and mayonnaise is splashing on your plate. Here's what I'm learning about the surprisingly good taste of failure.

1. FAILURE HELPS YOU FOCUS

FIRST iZ has taught me that complex ideas fail when people get lost in the details, instead of focusing on the big picture and breaking it down into manageable steps. The view of your problems from 30,000 feet is very different—although I should say 400 feet since a drone cannot legally fly above that altitude! Ramping up FIRST iZ has reminded me that there's nothing wrong with backing up to see where you're headed and then figuring out the baby steps to solutions as you go along. Bite-sized chunks, remember?

It's like when parents are expecting their first child. They wonder when people will figure out that they don't actually know what they're doing. So much emotion washes over a new parent. When you're looking into your baby's eyes for the first time you want to know, "What did I just do here?" This is usually followed by "I have no idea what's going on," "I'm going to screw this up," and something along the lines of, "This is not going to end well."

I've relived this parenting experience over and over while counseling stressed out first-time dads at Genesis through the years. Trust me, I tell them, it will all work out. Somehow, you figure it out as you go. It's the same way in business and in life. You figure it out as you go, as long as you keep focused on where you're going.

I am not necessarily a long-term strategic planning fan. I don't advise planning much further than thinking about what you can do this week, month, or quarter because you're going to get overwhelmed by the enormity of all the pieces involved. You're likely going to get discouraged. If you want to do longer-term planning, do it in outline form to allow items to easily adjust, and then fill in the unknowns as you go. Consider the small steps that you can make today.

That's what SCRUM teaches you to do—to break down big tasks into small, bite-sized pieces. It's no coincidence that this is the same way you eat a Failure Sandwich, bite by bite. You take an eight-month project and measure it out into two-week sprints that break down into one-day objectives. If there's anything I'm decent at doing, it's taking what seem to be disparate concepts and figuring out how to put them together to accomplish a certain goal. When you know what you want in the end, you just start going down the list—filling in the thousands of pieces that must come together and work in harmony to achieve that goal.

When we're breaking down an enormous project like FIRST iZ into small steps, alá the SCRUM technique, I tell my team, "Let's just take one step. Let's figure out what we've got to do today." Otherwise, we'd be overwhelmed.

Go back, if you will, to the fact that I am inherently lazy. If I have to do something more than once, I want to figure out a way to make it more efficient, like the one-click trunking systems we were involved with at the start of my career. FIRST iZ rests on the idea of simplicity—the one-button capability of FIRST iZ is one of its major selling points. To get to that one-click by a human, there are thousands of behind the scenes things that must be checked and executed.

For example, take the guy in charge of the drones at your local sheriff's department who wants to deploy a drone during a water rescue mission. In the early days, he carried a rugged, waterproof case containing the drone in the back of his pickup truck or SUV and made his way through traffic to the scene. Once he was there, he unloaded, opened up the case, and began assembling the pieces of the drone. The pieces used to have to be screwed together, so it was a major improvement when click-in-place drone assembly came along. Click, click, click, and then he's able to fire it up. Minutes have passed, mind you, in this emergency situation so far. He's in the air no earlier than 20 minutes, best case scenario.

What our patent-pending FIRST iZ does is to turn these older, clunky ideas and strategies on their head and provide a much more efficient process. Our idea was to keep the bird assembled, ready to go, and calibrated in drone ports (like airports but much smaller-sized for drones). These drone ports are stationed in strategic locations around the country so that within 60 seconds or less of pushing a button, the drone is on its way to the mission. For very large-scale operations, we have more ports than drones. A drone can fly out on a mission, then land in an empty port to recharge and dump its stored data before making its way back home. Think of the ports like the Tesla super-charging stations that are strategically placed along highways.

Drones have come a long way

There are still hoops to jump through out there, and garnering public acceptance is one of them. Drones, like anything else, can be used for good or evil. It really made my blood boil when I saw drones being used in Italy to "shout" obscene commands for crowds to disperse and shelter in place in the beautiful but virtually empty cobblestone streets of one of its quaint villages at the onset of COVID-19. That's not the gospel message we're trying to get across to the general public about how useful drones can be. Instead, we've already identified at least five strategic areas where FIRST iZ can obviously add value: first responders; campus safety at colleges, prisons, and giant manufacturing plants; critical infrastructure like nuclear power plants, wind farms, and shipping ports; linear inspection of pipelines and powerlines; and hazardous waste monitoring.

In addition to public acceptance, the FAA in charge of civil aviation safety is also a challenge and somewhat of a wildcard. In the drone world, there are four fundamental FAA rules we live under. We cannot fly a drone above 400 feet—check, we don't need to do that. You cannot fly it over people without a parachute—cross that off the list. You cannot fly it at night—you can actually get acceptable waivers here, so we're not worried about that. And the holy grail is flying the drone BVLOS (Beyond Visual Line of Sight)—in other words, you must keep eyes on the bird.

I love the way somebody once put it to me regarding the FAA's general modus operandi when it comes to data-gathering for a new endeavor like FIRST iZ:

The FAA tells you to bring them a rock.

And you say, "Well, okay, but what kind of rock?"

The FAA says, "Just bring a rock."

And you hunt around and find a rock. You take it to them to look it over.

Then the FAA says, "That's not the rock we're looking for."

You repeat this maddening process 10 times before they say, "That's it! That's the rock we were looking for."

My philosophy is that trying to navigate the FAA's requirements is like living in the early days of aviation when barnstormers were taking to the skies and there were no rules. Then officials went to the other extreme with a host of regulations, like requiring physical observers each time a plane took off and landed. These guidelines relaxed over time, as aviation became more accepted in our society. Today we're busy gathering data, data, data to ensure the safety of the public at all times, and I sincerely believe we'll meet and exceed expectations with our drones.

Plans Are Not Sacred

Ironically, FIRST iZ happens to be conducting its research and development during the worldwide pandemic. My message to people figuring out their way in a post-pandemic world today is to ask a pretty simple question amid all the complexity: What did you learn from yesterday? And what are you doing today? Problems like COVID-19 help you focus on what's important.

I've spent my share of hours in long board retreats and endless meetings drafting three- and five-year plans. Remember, the best ideas fail because people get lost in the details, instead of breaking a vision into manageable steps. I've found that the strategic plan often becomes an excuse for what we *can't* do, rather than a game plan for what we *can* accomplish. We feel that we can't pivot to another plan when the information changes because we have a cast in concrete three-year plan that we worked so hard on and even bragged about publicly! Don't think about three years or even a year from now—think long and hard about today.

If you are going to set annual goals, do them with the understanding that you should review them every quarter and not fret if things need to change. That's a good word, especially when so much continues changing around us today. The modern world we find ourselves in exposes the weakness of holding too tightly to long-term strategic plans. As I say, I fully believe COVID-19 is not the last pandemic we will face. So consider this is a warmup, a learning season on how to be flexible. Disruption and discomfort can be good because they show you how to focus on a new way of doing things. Ironically, I began writing this book before COVID-19 began serving up Failure Sandwiches all over the world!

2. FAILURE SHOVES YOU OUT OF YOUR COMFORT ZONE

The pandemic was the kind of seismic disruption that forced people to dig deep and figure out a way to still do what needs to be done to conduct business, feed their family, and educate their kids. Hairstylists in restricted areas moved their businesses outside and snipped hair in parking lots. Grandmothers who never owned an iPhone learned how to do Zoom meetings with their grandchildren's teachers. Churchgoers finally learned the Church is not a building but a community of people who can continue to worship and meet online. We figured out early on in 2020 that there are going to be new ways of doing everything from here on out.

Those who took the "we have failed, so I'll sit on my

stump and pout, then cry" attitude have really failed. They were so debilitated by events that they ceased to put one foot in front of the other. Those who made it through looked for the new paths. Those folks may have done so kicking and screaming, but they eventually found ways to press forward.

Saudi Arabia – Plan B

I remember when we were scheduled to go to the Middle East on business three weeks after 9/11. We cancelled our plane tickets, but we still had a purchase order in hand and needed to figure out a way to install software for a large, high-profile trunking system customer in Saudi Arabia. We stayed up many nights in a row here in the US, shifting around all our protocols and rewriting how to do business to meet this challenge.

There was no such thing as real broadband in 2001, so the team in Saudi Arabia ended up binding four DSL lines together to act as one bandwidth segment that would allow us to install the software. There was no Facetime, no Zoom, and no WhatsApp. There were no phone calls, only emails and the live typing on their computers from our office in Texas. I remember typing training instructions on their screen in Microsoft Notepad and entering accounts into our software in real time to show our clients halfway around the world how it worked. This was the first time we did a totally remote installation under those conditions, but we proved to our customers and to ourselves that it could be done. What I'm saying is that if you look hard enough, you can find solutions to most problems. Figure it out as you go and get out of your comfort zone.

FIRST iZ is, to me, symbolic of what it means to finish well and run the race, completing whatever task your purpose is on Earth. Whatever your thing is, whatever your "FIRST iZ" is, do it to the best of your ability. But if there's one thing we're learning with the launch of the FIRST iZ drone system, the road to success is not a straight path, and it's not a smooth ride. If you have no experience with speed bumps or potholes in your life, you're not going to have a clue what to do when you inevitably come across them. And you're not going to be able to lead others safely and successfully around them like we were able to do for this client. Try not to complain when you encounter trouble along the way to the top. You're learning valuable lessons here.

3. EARLY FAILURE TEACHES YOU WHAT YOU NEED TO KNOW

One of my children totaled several cars in a row as a teenager. I always say that I'm glad they got those out of the way early! It's no coincidence that this child hasn't had any accidents since! If you're going to fail, do it early and often. Find out all that you need to know now. Early failures will help you know what to do when you're further down the line and the stakes are much higher.

If you fail early in a project as complex as FIRST iZ,

that's the best thing that can happen to you. Why is that? You can deal with a lot of things if they happen early on. I remember running 200 to 500 cycles per week to try to get the system to fail. Test your stuff over and over— your theories, your products, your software. Stress test it and get it to fail early to tell you everything you need to understand before you go to market with the idea.

As I write this, SpaceX experienced what appeared to the world to be a massive failure of their Starship in Boca Chica, Texas. It flew great but had a thud-level landing. Here's what a SpaceX spokesman said: "With a test such as this, success is not measured by completion of specific objectives but rather how much we can learn, which will inform the probability of success in the future as SpaceX rapidly advances development of Starship." Translation: we'll get it right the next time (or the next time) because we learned so much from this failure!

In the case of FIRST iZ, we had a mechanical failure inside an early design of our drone port. It was like a scene from *Apollo 13* when our teams in Idaho, Texas, and at the port itself were trying to diagnose the problem. We were all looking at images and screens trying to get a closer look at what went wrong. It turned out that a bearing had shifted just enough to cause the failure. Whew!

We all agreed we preferred to find that out now rather than later when the drone is in the field. We changed to a different type of bearing, and that fixed the issue. Again, failure is your friend here. The more failure you experience early on, the smarter you will be when it comes to high stakes strategizing and decision-making. And, I might add, spend 99% of your time identifying what failed and how to prevent that failure and less than 1% on who caused it.

What partnerships can teach you

This principle applies not only to your idea but also to the people and partnerships you need to make it happen. As you can imagine, FIRST iZ is drawing together a very complex web of investors and players who are intent on changing the world through this technology. I'm embarrassed to say that in years past as a novice businessman I made business deals on my own without advisors and without attorneys. I trusted people because I knew they could trust me. I learned the hard way when the partnerships did not work out like I hoped.

I'll tell you an example.

I entered a partnership in the early Nineties without knowing the first thing about partnerships—how to create or maintain them. I just knew I needed money, and someone was willing to invest in my idea. Sound familiar to anyone? In the end, the company ended up being not viable, and we ended up parting ways. To bring that full circle, in the past 10 years I have tried to find the company and the man who invested in us so I could pay him back, but alas, all I can find is that he has passed away.

I've since learned that many partnerships are fraught with "I just need money" kind of statements. Oh, it may well be wrapped in other words, without necessarily declaring the fact that they need money to survive! Partnerships are too often formed by leaders in survival mode who don't take the time to think through what they're doing. You need someone who is experienced to guide you through your first and your next partnership—don't wing it.

If you're new in business and broke, you might not have the funds to hire who you need. Whether it's a lawyer down the street or a friend from school—it's important to put together a network of experienced people who can guide you through the business side of partnerships. You can also join online community groups like LinkedIn for free advice.

Then when you're successful and earning money, be sure to "dance with the one who brung ya," as we like to say in Texas. Reward those who helped you in the days when you could not help yourself. At some point, you may also find that you've hit the top level of what some of your early advisors can provide for you. Prepare in advance to move on to more capable and powerful help for the rest of your journey.

Partnerships go bad. I've had more than my fair share of experience there. And as much as I hate agreements, I've learned to embrace them. I have bulletproof agreements these days that cover all the ifs, ands, and buts. What if a partner dies? What if a partner divorces? What if one of you becomes incapacitated? There are all kinds of contingencies. One partnership agreement recently grew from 15 pages to over 80 pages when we were finished, and it cost a lot of money to produce it. Did I say already how much I hate agreements? But I have found they are very useful not just at the beginning of a new partnership but also to benchmark and guide daily operations and address problems when they come up. And they will come up.

There is a temptation when you run a business to think solely about yourself and the welfare of your own family. That's right and natural. But if you want to create something that lasts long past you, you must think far beyond that. What happens to the company once you're gone? Agreements help answer that question. They memorialize all the "set up the partnership" conversations you have into one place.

Phirst Technologies, LLC, (the company that houses FIRST iZ) has a lot of partnerships. I have a new agreement right now with another businessman, and I have no doubt we can work out any problem that may arise. If it were just the two of us, it would be fine to have some simple documentation in place. But we both know we must write an agreement as if we don't exist. The document should think forward to whoever is next in line to carry on the work because we're creating companies that will help change the way the world works. The agreement must be thought of in that light.

I failed early and often in this respect. But I learned exactly what I had to do to protect the investment of other people, as well as my own investment, when entering partnerships and agreements. Total transparency: I think all this learning has cost me a million dollars in fees over the past 30 years. Now that I have the opportunity to be responsible for much more of my own money and that of other people, I am much more prepared, careful, and a bit nervous to be honest!

4. FAILURE SHOWS YOU NEW OPPORTUNITIES

One of the reasons I hope my story helps people become more comfortable with problems and failure is to take away some of the stigma associated with it. People can handle a lot more than they believe they can endure. Coronavirus also taught us this important lesson.

At the start of the pandemic, no one could imagine that people and businesses would still be afloat a year or more later. People are more resilient than we often think. Riding out the scariest waves of stress will teach you a lot about the depths of your own strength.

Oh, be sure that I realize many have experienced catastrophic change because of COVID-19, either directly or indirectly. Still, as I have said many ways in this book, we all have two fundamental ways to react when failure and tragedy happens. We can hold onto a "woe is me" attitude and collapse, or we can be energized to find a new way to forge ahead.

I believe more people will become entrepreneurs post-pandemic than ever before. Not only have people learned that they can come through hard times and make it to the other side, but also they've discovered new skills and interests they didn't know they had. Some people have discovered a spark of entrepreneurship inside, and they're stepping out into new ventures they never would have considered otherwise. Some accidental entrepreneurs were born in 2020 because they lost their jobs, which forced them to come up with something else to do. And the really creative types will come up with something that's not just good for next week to pay the bills, but also something that is good for the next five years.

When oil plunged to a dollar per barrel, a friend of mine transitioned from 15 successful years of working in the oil fields to the wild frontier of entrepreneurship. He looked around during the pandemic for opportunities and asked, "What do people really need during this time?" He and I kicked around ideas, and he began knocking on some doors. Then he worked up some prototypes and kept pushing and working at it until he had a breakthrough. Now he's on the cusp of a very successful business using artificial intelligence to address public safety and health. His pioneering story is being repeated in various industries throughout the world.

I'll tell you another example. When we started Tyler

Innovation Pipeline (TIP) in 2017, we had no idea that out-of-work people in 2020 would come to our full-time maker space to explore making their product ideas come to life. TIP has 3D printers, a laser engraver, ShopBot, a green screen and podcast room, and all the software to make it work. We have the tools to go from an idea to promoting a product. Members can access over $300,000 worth of equipment, all for a reasonable monthly membership fee.

It is ideal for a post-pandemic world! Our current rock star is a man who just had a patent granted on a small device he created while at TIP. How many other people out there are bound and determined to change directions and give their dreams a shot?

There's no mythical "one right path"

When you're studying your options and looking for opportunities, I hope you'll realize that there is not just one allowable path. I have learned by experience that God has the ability to bless a lot of options, if you put him in the driver's seat of your life. Many people resign themselves to fate and rule out many things that could have actually worked in their favor. They look at a possible new job opportunity, for example, and think, "Well, that's never going to happen because it's just not my destiny." So they never pursue it. Or they mess up royally on a business venture—and they think it's all over, so they quit trying altogether to follow their dreams.

To a large degree, I think you can make your own destiny. Follow along with me here. Your particular life experience and personal make-up will rule out some things for you. If you're not a math and logic person, you're likely not going to go into computer programming, right? (But it could happen.) And if you're a couch potato, you're likely not going to be a professional long distance runner. (But it's possible.) The aggravation for me is when people rule out what they don't want to do, or aren't equipped to do, and then they wait for destiny to reveal the "one" thing they are really meant to do.

I had a calling early in life. But I also had a lot of freedom within that calling to work it out over several decades.

Many people, however, are too impatient. They want life to knock them upside the head and tell them what they're supposed to do next. They want the answers written very clearly on a billboard or handprinted across the sky. Here's a radical thought: If you are a believer, and you're sincerely trying to follow what God wants for your life, God can bless any of your decisions. You get to choose.

Oh, man, how 'bout that! That's exactly what we don't want to hear because it puts the choice back on us! Again, God can bless any of that when you're so in love and so in tune with him that you understand how he's moving and leading you. He can even work with failure.

I have visited with many men who are busy fretting

over a career change—especially when getting a new job wasn't their idea, if you know what I mean. I can't tell you the number of them who have said to me, "I don't know what to do. I never learned anything else besides (insert career here)." Sometimes I just want to shake them to wake them from their stupor. Why is it too late to learn something new? My friend Bernie May is 88 at the time of this writing, still maintains his pilot's license, and just started a for-profit bee business! Now tell me again, what is your excuse?

After I listen to the stories of these often-depressed men in my office recliner, I advise them to take a little time (very little time) to get over the emotion of the job loss. At first, they're often in an emotional state where logic just won't help. You cannot win an emotional argument with logic. People need a little white space to grieve what's gone. After a week or so, we can meet again and speak logically about helping them see their options.

I recommend doing a post-mortem of every failure you experience. Do the hard work of sitting down and asking yourself, "How did that happen?" And, "What can I do different next time?" Many times, just getting these men to talk helps remind them of the other talents and capabilities they own that they forgot about. And they see how failure opens new opportunities.

MAKING FAILURE WORK FOR YOU, NOT AGAINST YOU

In business, we have lengthy strategy discussions about

all the potential outcomes when we're trying to make important decisions. We can look at a list of pros and cons behind every option, but in the end, I believe you go with your gut, based on the good and bad parts of your history. You draw on what you've learned through prior successes and failures. Then you plug in that information to see how a certain option is going to turn out. Thomas Edison famously remarked that he hadn't failed in his initial attempts to invent the light bulb, he'd just discovered 10,000 things that didn't work.

In coding software, we use tons of what we call IF/THEN decision trees. IF certain conditions exist, THEN a resulting action follows. And, there is also ELSE. ELSE is typically reserved for a condition that is not covered by the IF/THEN. Adding // means a comment follows. Example:

IF CLOCK() >=0500 .and. <=1200
THEN // **It's morning**
          Drink coffee
ELSE// **It's afternoon**
          Drink something non-caffeinated
ENDIF

(NOTE for the programmers: I've added the THEN and ELSE statement for reader clarity. You would not normally need or use them if the code is properly created.)

In life, it works the same way. IF you go down a certain path, THEN you will encounter certain results. Sometimes they're the kind of results that you want—and sometimes they're not. With practice, you learn to take a different path in the future that leads to better results. That's perhaps the biggest lesson that failure can teach you.

LET ME ASK YOU SOMETHING

Have you been calling the waiter over to send all the Failure Sandwiches back to the kitchen because you don't like them? Or are you making your way through each one, bite by bite, determined to learn something from every single one?

Maybe you have a messy family history like The Sloppy Joe. Get another napkin and keep chewing. That can't hold you back unless you let it. You may be making your way through a B-L-T, wondering if there's anything meaningful to the order of your life events so far. Don't get impatient—you'll look back and start connecting all the random dots.

Maybe you're in the middle of The Grinder years— and you're about to burn out from all the long hours at the office. Keep at it. Take one more bite. And hey, you may not know EXACTLY what's under all that cheese in The Patty Melt—it might be unappetizing, to say the least. There are going to be good days and bad days, green lights and red lights, no matter what. That's life.

The Colossal? Now, that is a tough one—rejection doesn't get any easier the older you get. Negativity and discouragement are everywhere. Glance around and you'll see others sitting in life's deli working on their own version of The Colossal. And when (not "if") you have the misfortune of making your way through life-altering change (a.k.a. The Seven-Year Ick), remember I'm pulling for you. Regardless of which Failure Sandwich is on your plate right now, don't let it get in the way of what you are called to do with your life.

There are times when you'll be tempted to order The Looky Loo for someone—pointing fingers at their failure and saying, "I told you so!" I hope you'll make a better choice and help someone else through their mistakes and misfortunes. If you have a bitter taste in your mouth from a Regret on Rye, don't stop there. There is a sweeter, better day coming in your future if you'll promise me one thing and not give up. Maybe you're like me, with both hands wrapped around The Double Decker Doozy—not only losing one role but also gaining another as you transition through life's inevitable stages on a business and personal level. You'll likely make a lot of mistakes at this point. But see it through to the end, despite the number of failures and mishaps you endure.

The ONE sandwich I omitted is the Philly Cheesesteak! I grew up where that icon originated, so don't fault me for not being able to bring myself to name it a failure. I often remind Bobbie that for the rest of my life, I am on the "Phil's Disappointing Philly Cheesesteak Tour," since nothing comes close to matching up to the real deal! There's got to be a life lesson in that, so tell me sometime what you come up with.

Whatever life serves up at this particular moment, let my story remind you to keep at it. Jesus said it well. "Whoever can be trusted with very little can also be trusted with much, and whoever is dishonest with very little will also be dishonest with much. So if you have not been trustworthy in handling worldly wealth, who will trust you with true riches? And if you have not been trustworthy with someone else's property, who will give you property of your own?" (Luke 16:10-12)

JUST SHOW UP

I have referred to the great book *DRIVE*, by Daniel Pink, several times. The core principle he works with is that most every human has a desire to make a mark on the world. We are listening for that inner voice to say, "I created that!" Not everyone has a desire to make their mark for good, of course. Take the kid that creates crude graffiti; he's making his mark on his neighborhood, but not for good. Redirecting that talent, he could be creating murals that would be applauded by the masses. For years I told our programmers that I wanted their names in the "about" box inside our software so the world could see who was responsible for the great products we have. Things like this are your fingerprints. You want others to look at your work and see your fingerprints on it to know you had something to do with its creation.

My fingerprints are all over Genesis. And if you look close enough, you see a little bit of Sloppy Joe and some leftover Patty Melt around those prints. My fingerprints have a little scarring from the failures I've written about, and others that we'll save for another time. But my prints are there. How about yours?

Is it conceivable that God can use all your past failures to prepare you for more responsibility in the future? In my case, I would say so. And remember this—I don't think I'm that interesting! There may be many more people far more interesting than I am. But as someone wisely reminded me, it's really not my story. It's God's story, and I just happened to show up (thanks again, Bernie!).

And that's my best advice to you—show up. Keep going. Don't quit. By God's grace, an uninteresting man like me, with a lot of help from hundreds of great people, built a multi-million-dollar global business. Imagine what wonderful things he could be up to in your life. And who knows? All the uninteresting people like us might just make the world a better place...one bite at a time.

Story Index

Chapter 1 – The Sloppy Joe
NYC Deli items
Phil's Life Failures.doc
Dad and Mom in Chester
I discover the truth about my family
Willie goes to prison
WCHR tour and TWR Bonaire
Mr. Winder talks about Texas

Chapter 2 – The B-L-T
LETU campus radio jobs
"Aaaand you're going to hell...."
Hacking the LETU phones
Longview central telephone office escapade
Building KHYM-AM
Working two stations at the same time
National Gospel DJ Contest
"Flooders"
Hiring on at KLTV-TV
Earl Campbell – the interview that never was
Encountering a head-on collision

Memories of a weekend anchor
Moody Broadcasting – I want to be a missionary
Called to send, not to go

Chapter 3 – The East Texas Grinder
Getting stuck, installing phone lines for Piggy
Meeting at Radio Shack
Motorola offers me a job
Let's build a tower—and other bright ideas
Ta da! The TRS-80
Blowing Irene's mind
What is "time" anyway?

Chapter 4 – The Patty Melt
Jenny and Mandy's birth
Jecca Towers
Cashflow anyone?
Tales of EZBill
Meet Nextel
A line in the sand with Bobbie, Ally, and Josh
Third smartest thing I've ever done in my life
A new beginning – Genesis
The Batman Building
A big sale to Nextel
EZBill built-in noises—this stuff really works!
First international sale, Australia
Any Key?
Where's the power button?
Is that really coffee?
God Loves You – EZBill in Ecuador
An unexpected gardener in a blue jumpsuit

The Mack truck syndrome
Motorola break up

Chapter 5 – The Colossal
Miss Yoder
Playground blues
The Nutcracker, not so suite
The Power of Words list
Telling close friends what they mean to you
Neil and Nels
Motorola is back on

Chapter 6 – The Seven-Year Ick
Experiencing God?
CB radio blues
A letter in my desk
IDATel and the Taliban
Spyder on the Interstate
Sell Genesis?
Mom's death
The family that sings together
My stage debut
Shaking the hand of a millionaire
Just changing addresses

Chapter 7 – The Looky Loo
Building the Tesla coil
Bernie May, a passionate man
Don't give up on someone
Grace is enough – a lesson in mercy
Why is the grass greener?
Tax miscalculation—a priceless experience

Chapter 8 – The Regret on Rye
No money in the bank
Jakarta calling
IRSgate
Three jars for money
Full kimono in relationships
A man flying in a helicopter
Rebanding launches Genesis to the next level
Dreaming a dream
How not to get a bank loan
Starting over even better
Award-winning architecture

Chapter 9 – The Double Decker Doozy
Spyders—the ultimate empty nest glue
An email I did not expect
A dark weekend
Changing my role at Genesis
Rocks are just below the surface
Genesis PULSE
FIRST iZ comes on the scene

Chapter 10 – When Failure Tastes Good
FIRST iZ at an accident
The FAA tells you to get a rock
Kingdom of Saudi Arabia, Plan B
Failing early—500 cycles later, what we learned
Business partnerships go awry
COVID-19 and the birth of more entrepreneurs
Tyler Innovation Pipeline
Is there just one path?
If/Then and Now What?

About the Author

P hil Burks is the Founder and CEO of Burks GenCore Co., Inc.; GenCore Candeo, Ltd.; GenCore International, Ltd.; GenCore, LLC; MBCG, LLC; and Phirst Technologies, LLC. Shortly after graduating from LeTourneau University with a bachelor's degree in Electrical Engineering Technology, Phil Burks began a rising career in sales with Motorola. An oilfield client offered a new position and opportunity for Phil to start a tower rental company, and in 1980 Jecca Towers was born. Jecca owned towers and sold and installed towers for MCI, AT&T, and various communication firms. In 1988 Motorola purchased Jecca Towers, and The Genesis Group began.

In 1989, Genesis grew from a single DOS-based billing software product that Phil wrote in his bedroom, to now over 30 Windows and browser-based software products that are designed to enhance Motorola critical two-way radio systems. Genesis software is globally installed for clients including: Motorola Australia, The Kingdom of Saudi Arabia, Bell Mobility Canada, the States of Florida, Virginia, Louisiana, Arkansas, Illinois, South Carolina, Cities of New York, San Francisco, and many others. Genesis has grown to include over 60 full time employees at their Tyler, Texas, office; an office in London; and close affiliates in Melbourne and Mexico City. In April 2013, Phil stepped down as president to remain owner and CEO of the software enterprises. Most recently, along with another tech entrepreneur, Phil created and is the managing member of Phirst Technologies, LLC, to develop and market a specialized drone for police, fire, and ambulance called FIRST iZ (pronounced First Eyes). More information on the software portion of Phil's pursuits can be obtained at https://www.genesisworld.com, https://firstiz.co and www.GenesisPULSE.com. His real estate development pursuits and additional information can be obtained at www.CorporateGreenTyler.com.

Phil has served on many local non-profit boards, including as a founding member of Tyler Innovation Pipeline, www.TylerInnovators.com and as a trustee at LeTourneau University in Longview, Texas, www.LETU.edu. Phil and his wife, Bobbie, make their home in Tyler, Texas.

Additional Resources

For bulk purchasing options, as well as bonus material and information about the book, visit the publisher at www.philburks.com or email sales@philburks.com.

For information regarding the availability of author speaking engagements, email author@philburks.com for booking details.